RIDE IT!

The Complete Book of

MOTORCYCLE TOURING

Ken Craven 1977

First published April 1977

All rights reserved. No part of this book may be reproduced or transmitted in any form or by any means, electronic or mechanical including photocopying, recording or by any information storage or retrieval system, without permission in writing from the copyright holder

Printed and bound in England by the publishers

Published by
The Haynes Publishing Group
Sparkford Yeovil Somerset BA22 7JJ England

a FOULIS MOTORCYCLING BOOK — ISBN **0 85429 223 3**

Editor Jeff Clew
Production/Design Tim Parker with Annette Cutler
Illustration Terry Davey

The Haynes Publishing Group

distributed in the USA by
Haynes Publications Inc
9421 Winnetka Avenue
Chatsworth
California 91311 USA

RIDE IT!

The Complete Book of

MOTORCYCLE TOURING

Ken Craven

Contents

Dedication

I am merely one of the many who has dedicated a book to his wife but none could have done so with more justification. She is a journalist and writer of recognised ability and, being a skilful typist, has been of the utmost assistance in the preparation and revision of this work, as well as correcting my frequently erratic spelling.

Of more importance was her participation in the history of the subject matter, when she was sentenced to the barbaric and prolonged cruelty of being exposed to wet, intense cold or intense heat for hours on end, in an undernourished state. For full measure she has been cast by me to the ground on mud or boulders.

The rare moments when she complained were always made tolerable by the original use and combination of profanities in several languages, when English failed her. Only a few times did she threaten to walk out on me forever — the fact that she never did so is proof she has the soul of a saint and martyr. So with heartfelt thanks I dedicate this book to my wife, Mollie, without whose endurance this book could never have been written.

Ken Craven

Introduction

This is a book for the road rider, the person who uses a motorcycle for functional transport or weekend pleasure jaunt or combination of both. Even more, it is a book for the tourist and adventurer who goes far afield on two wheels. It is also a book for the man (or woman) who has never ventured more than 20 miles from home, but who would have the time of his life if he could but be persuaded to try it and see.

The motorcycle is the ultimate of man's achievement in the creation of the personal human conveyance. Those two wheels with an engine in the middle are as near as you will get to a motive force which you will actually wear, or at least until the invention of clip-on wings! You ride a bike, it becomes part of you — not a thing you sit in and drive. You will be wafted through the air with a real sense of movement, vision is unrestricted and the changing scene becomes intimate and real. You are not observing it through a glass window — you belong.

These thoughts are not original. T.E. Lawrence (of Arabia) resorted to equally lyrical phrases about motorcycling. Yet even so, my feelings are my own discoveries, as they have been for countless others.

All this may sound hackneyed, churned out from habit after four decades of involvement in motorcycling. But in all truth, my enthusiasm for each new motorcycling adventure is enlarged rather than diminished through knowledge gained through experience. It is my hope now (and hope is modest enough) that my knowledge may be of benefit to others and that my experience will provide a little inspiration as well as entertainment.

Acknowledgements

No book is the work of one man, and when it comes to the photographs and illustrations, it could involve dozens. Such is the case with this book. I should like to thank all those who have contributed. To those who are not mentioned, please forgive me, I have been unable to trace the fact that you may be the originator of a particular illustration.

Thank you, in alphabetical order, Barclays Bank Limited, Belstaff Limited, Les Brazier, Churchgate Mouldings Limited, *Cycle World,* Kawasaki Motor Corporation, USA, *Motorcycle Sport,* The Music House (Sherborne), B. R. Nicholls, Neilsons Chemists (Ilchester), Tim Parker, Bruce Preston, The RAC, Rickman Brothers Limited, Ridgeway Feature Press, Servu (Yeovil), Sportography, Stadium Limited, Tower Products Limited, and John Wright.

Author Ken Craven astride his equipped Honda CB500 Four just prior to his departure for the 1976 *Motorcyclist Illustrated* Monte Carlo Rally

1 Let's go!

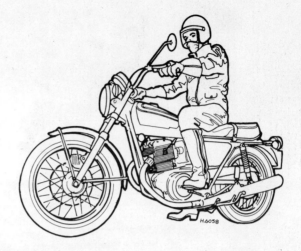

The most vivid memory of my childhood was the happening of my eighth birthday, for this was liberation day, the occasion of my first bicycle. Probably I was too adept at being able to balance the thing right from the start as liberation was postponed for enforced tuition, consequent on my bowling over the Chairman of the Great Western Railway during my first experience of descending a steep hill.

Shortly after this postponement, I pedalled off to visit my brother at his boarding school, the best part of 100 miles distance, and all in a day. My adventures on two wheels had begun. It was the most wonderful machine in the world, almost, and all that was now required was a little engine which would push it along effortlessly, just a bit faster than I could pedal. Then it really would be the most wonderful machine in the world.

Fundamentally, my views have not changed. If one has a motorcycle of any shape or size, providing it will hold together, well, you have a vehicle for conquering the globe and all you need now is the time and the money. The point I want to make....the thing I want all young people of any age to get excited about until they can't bear to wait to set off, is that a motorcycle, large or small, is the superb unrivalled tool for providing more sheer joy per minute than anything else. Yet this enjoyment will be further multiplied if the rider is equipped also with a certain measure of basic knowledge: the advantage of prior planning, what luggage is essential and what is merely a nuisance; what to look out for and what to avoid. That is the purpose of this book, to pass on as much as possible of what I have learned in the years of travel in my own home country of England and a portion of the rest of the world besides.

I have declared that any size of machine will do and I suppose I must modify this by stating the minimum which I would find tolerable for a long journey. If nothing else were available within my income, I would settle for a moped able to maintain a cruising speed of 30 mph on level ground, and able to cope with steep hills without pedal assistance. Modern motor vehicles have distorted our sense of proportion relating to speed. 30 miles an hour means a two minute mile, 44 ft per second, which is six times faster than a brisk human gait: it means 200 miles per day without undue fatigue, given average conditions. What's wrong with that, young people, before you are spoiled by road burners? I must confess that my experience with mopeds has been confined to a few short runs with different models but back in the early 60's I undertook a fairly long test trip with a 98 cc Triumph Tina scooter, which could be coaxed to a doubtful maximum speed of 45 mph on level road when at this speed, it gulped petrol. The Tina was not a commercial success and its name has long been forgotten. Nevertheless, it carried me 440 miles on the first day out from the channel port to Switzerland, thence to the Bavarian Alps in Germany, on through Austria to Italy and back again to Switzerland, over three major mountain passes. All this in 5 days (4 nights) and without my feeling unduly fatigued.

Although I find enjoyment in little bikes and the challenge of wringing the best performance out of them, my own choice has been for heavy calibre machinery even though, from my point of view, I feel that many have become too heavy and complicated in recent years.

I have already made the point that any machine with two wheels and something to push it along is crying out to be used. But this isn't the same thing as saying that all are equally suitable for all purposes. The Superbike is most at home on super highways but is likely to be at a disadvantage to the middle range and lightweights in narrow congested streets or over rough surfaces and twisting mountain roads. Nor must it be assumed that with a Superbike one can go further with less effort and fatigue than the smaller models which bear some comparison.

Wisconsin Country Kitchen—Ken samples an MV Agusta fitted with his original design of panniers

This time New Jersey forms the backdrop to Ken on a friend's fully restored Vincent Black Shadow

Hardly a machine for long distance touring. Ken demonstrates his versatility by riding this Batavus moped through the streets of Toronto

This is a common fallacy and I cannot blame anyone for making this mistake as I did so myself for a long while. In the early years of organising group tours I insisted on a minimum capacity of 350 cc (which in those days produced a great deal less power than its modern counterpart). Finally I was persuaded, a little reluctantly, to accept riders with comparatively underpowered scooters. Did they hold everyone else up? — on the contrary, again and again it was the little ones that arrived first at the day's destination, their riders being washed and spruced up by the time the first of the road burners arrived. How come? Slower riders are more aware that you cannot make up for lost time and also when riding at a modest speed there is less reason to have prolonged rest stops to stretch and ease tired shoulder muscles. But the owners of the big ones assumed that with their extra speed they could always catch up. They overlooked that the time eventually comes....sooner than the Superbike rider expects....when even the speed of light would not be enough for them to catch up. The little ones would already be there.

I am not here concerned with influencing the choice of machinery and I doubt if I could with anyone who is not a novice — after a few years motorcyclists become inflexible about their likes and dislikes and become very

What better background than the Grand Canyon, Ken and passenger get off their R60/5 BMW to take in the view

firm about what they want. 'You pays your penny and you takes your choice, and what you have will do fine, even if the size of your purse has scaled down your ultimate ambitions.

I have dealt in a generalised sort of way about the steed....what are the requirements of those who ride them?

No one will pretend that the motorcycle is the most comfortable form of transport. They can, let us face it, be downright misery at times. If it is comfort one is seeking, one goes by car or plane. But adventure and heightened pleasure come from contrast; from the difficulties being met and overcome. The dedicated traveller by motorcycle requires a certain minimum standard of physical fitness. It is not a matter of muscle, but more of resilience and durability. In my many years of experience it is my impression that the ones who adapt the quickest, suffer the discomforts best, respond to the good days with the most enthusiasm, are the young ladies perched up behind on the dual seat.

Few, if any, motorcyclists positively enjoy riding through endless rain; there have been occasions at night with many miles still to cover when it has been my idea of hell, which goes on and on, apparently for all time. Yet there will be rain that has been ridden through at times on most tours. You must have a sense of humour, and the ability to press on, cursing every long minute of it....and then later, including among your favourite stories to share with your fellow travellers, "that dreadful day when it rained without a break and it got into my boots until they filled with the stuff". Nobody except a masochist could possibly like it at the time. The motorcyclist will survive it. And as experience grows, the tourist will begin to relish it in a cussed kind of way "it is so extra beautiful when it stops". Sure enough, no sun shines brighter, more warmly and cheerfully, than the one which breaks through in glorious splendour after a bad day.

If that is you now, or if you think you might become such a person — or would like to have a try — then you are the stuff of which long distance motorcyclists are made.

In no way can you hang panniers on a chopper!

A Honda Monkey Bike is no machine to ride out of town; Ken attempts to leave New Jersey the hard way

Forclaz pass just after the war. Then it had a loose surface of the type shown

2 Where to?

THE ART OF PLANNING OR MAKING A TRIP LAST SIX MONTHS

I cannot begin to guess at the percentage of folk with a motorcycle in the stable who use them imaginatively for journeys outside their usual beat but, judging from the numbers to be seen on the open road, it can hardly be the majority. Even so, it is likely that most owners will succumb to the sudden urge to get up and go when the sun shines brightly and the forecast is set for fine. And how many give advance thought to planning for the contingency? Not many I'll bet, to judge by the popular choice of most road users at weekends for the great arterial highways that run from the cities to the resorts. Forgive me, if I appear to be speaking down to people as from on high. After all, I did the same thing on snap excursions myself, when I was younger, seldom bothering much about the alternatives to the obvious which, of course, were also obvious to everyone else.

The happiest and most successful trips are generally the best planned ones. This applies no less to the spur-of-the-moment day trips as presumably the alternatives will have received some consideration in advance and been stored away in the memory bank. What a pleasant way to pass a winter evening, when there is little on the television that appeals, for few people are immune to the pleasures of anticipation. Of more importance still is the planning of a journey of greater duration, to an area outside of one's previous experience. Without adequate preparation, it could be a disaster or, if not that, it is certain it will fall far short of its potential.

To cite the classic example of inadequate planning; how do the majority of my fellow motorists (I use the term to embrace all types of motor vehicles) set about plotting their first tour on the continent of Europe? I am not here concerned with the documentation involved or choice of transport across the Channel, which is dealt with in the concluding section. The idea itself is not likely to be spontaneous but one which has finally materialised after a long period of gestation, perhaps years. There will be preconceived notions about the many places to visit, which will have been formulated from early childhood and the result will be a lot of names of places or particular areas. Nine out of ten (and I can't vouch for the precise statistic) will then join up these names with the thickest, boldest lines that appear on the map. If they do this, they will find themselves with a hundred thousand boxes on four wheels, scurrying along day after day over wide expanses of asphalt wasteland which look so very like the equivalent highways in most parts of the world. They will have the same familiar filling areas for vehicles as well as humans, at top prices for mass produced pap. For instance, the Great St. Bernard tunnel enables the motorist to go further, faster, and will undoubtedly spare him the delay of the long zig-zag climb over one of the most spectacular of the high Alpine passes. If he is alert to this and still chooses the tunnel, well and good. The tragedy is when the tourist takes the tunnel from force of habit, by selecting the quickest way, and fails to give real consideration to the alternative and what he is missing.

Apart from those with a single destination, the folk who want to see a lot of places and plan a circular tour, usually start off with only a vague knowledge of distances and try to take in too much. This is a mistake made by almost every beginner I have known, including myself — and I still continue to do it (on occasions)! It has two possible results. Either the traveller presses on, and completes his planned schedule, but does so at the price of repeatedly having to leave an area before he wanted to. Or he will dawdle to suit his inclinations during part of his itinerary and then be forced to abandon the rest because the time to return to work has caught up with him.

His journey may have been a successful one but it will have been decided for him rather than be the one of his own choice. Areas will have been omitted which he specifically wanted to visit.

Not a road sign to be met very often. If you do, you will be a long way from home. This is Mexico during Ken's BSA 650 and sidecar trip

Another mistake (if you will forgive the word: who am I to say what is right and what is wrong? What I mean is some thought or action likely to have a result that one did not wish or intend), is that the person who has linked place names together, has been thinking in terms of destination.

It is a common mistake because it is a natural one: most of one's travelling life is concerned with reaching destinations. In the morning it is one's place of work; and in the evening, one's home. Holiday brochures and advertisements are dominated by the idea: Majorca for sunshine: travel by....Airlines. See Naples and Fry.

So the most natural and normal thought for someone contemplating a motorcycle holiday is: "Where shall we go?" There is nothing wrong in this, so long as one realises what one is doing....and the implications. If the answer is "I want to go to Venice," then admirable....but is a motorcycle the best way of getting there? It certainly won't be the quickest or cheapest! The shortest distance between two points is spelled aircraft.

The touring rider may have to school himself deliberately, at least in his earliest days, into thinking: "I want to reach Venice, but to take a week or more in getting there, and getting as much as possible out of the roads, the scenery, the towns and villages, the local foods and wines, that lie between us."

The mistake, if I may again use that convenient word, does not lie in having destinations (they do save wandering aimlessly in circles) but in allowing one's self to be dominated by them, through habit, when what one really wants is a tour.

Old and new meet 6 kilometres from Lapac in Yugoslavia

Motorways, freeways, autostradas, or by any other name, were created to provide the conditions for rapid and safe transit between two points and Europe now has a massive network which can help one on one's way to a chosen area as well as linking places of particular interest. But you will never capture the 'feel' of a country on a motorway.

Motorways still constitute only a tiny fraction of Europe's roads, streets and byways, certainly less than 1%, so one must depart from these great concrete arteries and their international sameness to see how the other 99% live. After all, travel is largely about people. It is one thing to gaze in awe across a great range of snowcapped mountains which are as nature made them, but man does not thrive by views alone. One belongs to a human community and it is the cultivated fields on the slopes of the foothills, or the Alpine village that shelters in the folds that give reassurance, character and interest during the changing scene as one progresses.

Despite a steady trend towards an international way of life, of chrome fixtures, plastic furniture, instant foods that neither please nor offend. Shell and Coca Cola advertisements, self service stores where you select mass produced things of mediocre value made to look better than they are by fancy wrappings — people still manage to preserve some of their national character when they group together in their own surroundings.

Most small towns still have their communal or street markets where, among other things, you can buy

Winter touring in Switzerland can still be pleasant, especially with the attraction of skiing

Bullocks can prove an unexpected hazard, especially in Eastern Europe, and even worse at night

Sofia and you are never alone. Note the distances and the traffic policeman's 'wand'

A Partitour pauses high up in the Dolomites

Once everyone on a motorcycle could explore these mountain tracks. Today, machine limitations make it much more of a hazard

fruits and vegetables which were not all grown to a standard size to be wrapped in standard packets, where they are not only cheaper but also taste a lot better. Furthermore, you will be served by a human and not just a machine that spews out a ticket and your change controlled by an operator who does not see you as a person able to smile, crack a joke or respond in some way. And then there is the local pub, or cafe, bar or tavern (depending on the country). They are all so different and somehow remain different, even though the youth of the world, so conforming, all dress to the international fashion of the day. Alas, the national costume is now rather a thing of the past but at least the wearers speak their own languages and have their own gestures.

So, if you want to travel and not be a mere tripper, you should plan to escape from the main highways and the places they serve, for at least some of your time.

This is where imaginative planning comes in and, again, what better way could there be of enjoying a chill winter evening -- in fact, you could spend six months in happy anticipation. To do this, your first and indispensable requirement is a map — about which there will be more in the next section. Now let us assume you are setting off on your own which, of course, can mean with a wife or friend as passenger or perhaps with another tagging on behind, on their own machine. You will certainly have a destination or specific areas you wish to visit but, even so, you will not have to run to an exacting schedule, unless you have planned a marathon, which I do not advocate, when there is no pressing reason. You are now in the happy position of being able to keep your options open when it comes to the trip itself. This does not reverse the need for a plan but suggests the provision of alternatives. You may well have a definite plan to use motorways over a fair section, to be able to

The Acropolis in the background shows that Greece is not too far for the really adventurous

Not only the mountains hold an attraction for tourists. Towns and villages have their own special appeal

spend more time in other chosen areas — fine, but don't be too specific about your time schedule. What if it is one of those dreadful days of low, scudding cloud, poor visibility and drops of every size? You could well make a late start, or not at all, or an early finish. Or what if everything is beautiful and you are in fine fettle and able to pour on the miles? This is keeping your options open so far as timing is concerned. Why not, if you are a free agent?

As an example of this, Mollie and I undertake fairly frequent trips to the Spanish Costa del Sol, where we obtained a small villa in happier days when pounds were composed of shillings and a shilling could still buy something. Whenever we set off we have our route planned for the first day, and we endeavour to adhere to a pre-determined mileage which will see us well on our way, as we aim to complete the whole journey in five days travel (4 nights on the road) and have time to enjoy the rest of the 1,300 mile trip. We do not regard the journey as a mere routine, to be terminated as quickly as feasible — we could cut a day if we did. We seek as much variation as possible and there are many permutations open to us. Accordingly, after the first day we plan our route in stages and whether we decide to be exploratory over an untried road or select an express highway will depend on our energy, the weather and our whims, whatever they may be. This may seem an anti-plan approach, but not quite so. I would prefer to regard it as an open-plan tour, to give a new connotation to the expression. Bear in mind we are still trying to keep to an overall time table and we could not hope to adhere to it without having a very good idea of what each alternative is likely to entail — and whether it seems reasonable to calculate on making up time after a slow but scenic section.

For instance, we might decide when we are halfway down France to cross over the High Pyrenees instead of outflanking the mountain range at either end, but from then on, our choice of roads becomes more limited as we cannot afford to meander in wide, zig-zag deviations without greatly increasing our mileage. But there is still a choice which will then be influenced by the extent we have been delayed by our selection of mountain crossing. Of course, we consult maps on the way down but we are spared a prolonged study because we have previously undertaken an extensive map survey which, for this trip, includes the entire French/Spanish frontier from the Atlantic to the Mediterranean and from here a considerable section of Spain tapering down to our destination.

In coping with the basics of planning I have placed much emphasis on touring Continental Europe and this will continue to crop up throughout this book. But we are now very much part of Europe, even though our frontier is the most expensive stretch of water in the world — by which I mean, the cost per mile to cross it. Furthermore, my fellow Britisher does not need such extensive advice or guidance about touring in our own small islands, although much of the advice and information I am giving will, I hope, be of value when setting out to explore our own fair land. The same will apply to Americans and I would suggest to them that they do not act too literally on their age-old slogan 'See America First' because if they do this thoroughly, the very magnitude of it will occupy their vacations for much of their lifetime. The whole point of travel and adventure is variety and there is more of that to be found in Europe than any comparable stretch of land on this globe. To all the English speaking nations I would suggest they see Europe first or as soon as they can, as it will broaden their horizons and critical faculties.

Wherever you travel, close to home or very far afield, learn as much as you can about the places you are going to. Far from detracting from the adventure, it will make this more possible when you arrive there. It is not much of an adventure looking for a camping site for miles on end of industrial Zurich when you thought that all Switzerland was composed of mountains. This sort of silly error is so easy to make by the time a person has forgotten all his school geography. The time to revise your geography is when you are planning to go there, it then becomes a real live, fascinating topic. I've come back to the Continent again; right, Londoners, how much time would you devote to planning a two week camping tour in South West England. This is an area I know well and it is obvious to me that the vast majority of travellers have given it scant heed -- most of them are to be found on the same roads — which don't go through many of the interesting places.

For most people a holiday consists of a set time which must not be exceeded. If it is 16 days and they average as much as eight hours in the saddle (for an average that is a lot) that is still only 128 hours. If it is the hourly experience that matters, then each hour is worth planning for. It is your holiday. Enjoy it.

"Can you read a map?"

3 Can you read a map?

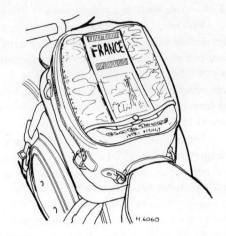

Everyone knows that, of course he can read a map! Towns are shown as blobs of various sizes, the bigger the blob, the bigger the town. Lines indicate roads; the thicker the line, the wider the highway. So why a whole section about map-reading?

I will start with an extreme, and recount what I managed to learn (by obligation rather than from choice at the time), using the Ordnance Survey maps produced under Government direction originally for military use — though now, in the 1 in 50,000 form, so popular that the smallest newsagent in the obscurest village in England may sell them.

During the last war, I rose to the heights of Sergeant Rifle Instructor in the Home Guard — and don't laugh about Dad's Army because we knocked the spots off the Grenadier Guards in shooting competitions at Bisley.

Map reading was a compulsory course for us NCOs. After all, if you have the task of attacking an enemy held farmhouse, your life and that of your platoon will depend on knowing where you will not make a perfect skyline target — **before** you get there.

Like industrial drawings, the principles of map reading are simple enough, but it takes practice, and often quite a prolonged study, to build up the complete mental outline in your mind. We were trained on the larger scale maps which show details down to individual buildings and are covered (as are the popular series) with thin wavy lines indicating the height, in steps of 25ft., I recall. With experience — and endless practice — we were able to extract from this plain sheet of paper a picture of the area which was not just like a photograph — it was a great deal better.

The touring motorcyclist does not need so much detail: indeed it can be an obstacle. The sheer cost of maps of the scale I have been mentioning, to cover only England, Scotland and Wales, probably runs into thousands of pounds! He will choose a much smaller scale; maps which cover a greater area for the same sheet size. Although much will be left out, a great deal will remain. I have in front of me a modestly priced Shell road map of S W England; a substantial area of territory. Yet it not only shows roads big, middling and small, cities, towns and villages, but also, by means of symbols, such things as viewpoints, castles, youth hostels, roadside telephone boxes, areas of oustanding natural beauty and much more.

It takes little instruction to understand all the symbols, and by themselves to find yourself immersed in an exciting mental exploration of the area. However, there is also much information which is not stated, but can be deduced, particularly if someone has given you a few hints as to the kind of thing to look for.

A map, for example, may show a peak close to the chosen route, of a height of 2,700 ft. Is that high or low? One then looks for a figure, or for some other sign from which a figure can be deduced, for the height of the road itself. If the road has been running steadily for some while at 2,600 ft, the peak may be reached and passed almost unnoticed; but if the road level is at 100 ft., it is likely to be spectacular.

Road levels are sometimes marked at intervals, but by no means always. They can, however, often be guessed. Rivers descend steadily from their source to the sea. If they are shown narrow in generally high country, the descent could be fairly rapid: when they broaden out, it is usually more modest. A road that is shown running adjacent to a river, therefore, will be at least close to the height of that river — not only at that point, but to the river height some distance before and after. If the road sticks very closely to the river, and meanders with it, one might ask why its builders did not shorten its length by making it straighter. Is there something that prevented them? — have we here a river flowing in a narrow gorge, between rocky and exciting heights?

Few maps show population density as such, but this too can easily be deduced. One area may be packed with dozens of small place names linked with innumerable little roads, to be followed by another where both roads and places thin out. What has happened? There will be a reason for this: one can be sure that a change has occurred in the nature of the terrain. Now one can find oneself devoting closer and closer study, with more and more imagination at work, trying to decide the nature of that change. Even if the outcome is a confession that one hasn't the slightest idea, at least the indication is there: when we reach this part of the tour, there will be some kind of change: watch out for it!

The planner will know that much has perforce been omitted from his map, and if he is attracted by the look of a small road that stops suddenly, just short of a highway that he wants to use himself, he may think: "The local population, too, will want to get through to the main road: probably there is a connection, only a small track which has been omitted from this particular map". Could be: it might be worth a try. But it is also worth looking very closely at the map, to see if there is some other reason for the road being cut short. It is surprisingly easy to miss, at first glance, something which is as clear as day once one has seen it. In this case, perhaps, a thin black line....denoting a railway line....in which case it is most unlikely that the assumed minor trackway will exist to link with the road. Railway builders don't like too many bridges, underpasses or level crossings.

I have now picked up a map which some readers may well already possess, and others may purchase if they intend to include France in a projected tour: a Michelin, covering the whole of France on one sheet, to a meagre scale of 1/1,000,000 or about 10 miles to 1 inch. If you happen to possess this or a similar map, may I suggest breaking off for a moment to go and fetch it, so that you can follow precisely the points I am about to make. If you haven't, don't worry; it really isn't essential.

The map still tells quite a story from direct reading, but there are difficulties in that the cartographers have been very mean with indicating altitudes....in fact they have only given figures for the principal mountain peaks. With these, it is easy enough to build a mental picture of the mountainous areas, tapering down to the foothills, by reading the figures for the peaks and noting the squiggly nature of the lines depicting roads engineered to lose substantial height without facing the traveller with impossible gradients.

But what about the forests and uncultivated lands depicted in green? Take, for example, that large slice of terrain south of Bordeaux, stretching south almost to Biarritz and south-east about halfway to Toulouse. The green indicates it is probably woodlands, which means it is also sparsely populated. But not necessarily....is it, in this case? On examining the map, we find far fewer roads and a scarcity of town names, compared with the entire surrounding region. So yes, it is surely sparsely populated. So, also, are mountain tops: could this be mountainous? Apart from the lack of figures for peak heights, there are several clues. The green area extends to the coast itself, which is shown as virtually a dead straight line right from the mouth of the Gironde to Biarritz. Mountainous coastlines are never dead straight! So this area is not uncultivated for that reason (and if this sounds like labouring the painfully obvious, remember that I am trying to call your attention to clues which can be helpful in cases where the answer may not be obvious at all).

Just inland from the coast, there are half a dozen large areas of water, most of them enclosed lakes. Above all, there is the river Gironde, with a massively wide estuary reaching practically to Bordeaux, and remaining a wide river for some distance beyond it. The picture that is beginning to emerge is one of land reclaimed by nature from the sea: flat and featureless and since it is not cultivated, certainly unsuitable for cultivation. Now I will tell you the truth. I have been there. It is flat, not a hill to be seen, obviously land reclaimed by nature from the sea and therefore perhaps once salt flats, though there is little of that now left, all very sandy and covered with pines....possibly man-planted. It is also pleasanter land than our deductions suggested, and there is no clue to be found in the map as to the quiet charm of its small townships.

This, I hope, will give you some idea of how much can be deduced where the map fails to give the specific information; and at the same time, show that with a road map such as this, one's deductions are unlikely to be 100% accurate.

As we have seen, apart from the definite information you can piece together from a map, a good deal more can be added through some inspired conjecture, with a fair chance you will be right. As a further instance, motorways frequently run very close to the former main roads which they have replaced, and it is probable that where the old road runs through open country, it will bear very little traffic and could be the preferred alternative. This I know to be true of the old Route National 5, 6 and 7 (same route, which changes its numbers on the way down), which runs from Paris to Marseille. This used to be known as the Widow's Route, because of its dreadful mortality rate, but is now a delightful road which weaves gently through a rolling landscape. It bears so little traffic that it is almost as fast as the adjacent Autoroute and is infinitely more interesting, quite apart from the useful saving of not having to pay a fairly hefty toll. Here, I grant, I am being wise after the event, relating to the section from Auxerre to Chalon, but it is a good bet that the same will apply to other long sections. On the other hand, where the former road links together a lot of towns in a dense area, it can be assumed that it continues to carry a lot of local traffic apart from the urban crawl in the towns themselves.

Another aspect of map reading/route selection, if you hold a ruler, north to south, east to west or whatever the direction of your travels are, main roads do not follow a consistently straight line but deviate along their course from town to town and weave about in between, depending on the topography, as road planners through-out history have tended to prefer the valleys or level areas. But look again along your rule and you will probably find that a combination of secondary roads follow a more direct line, and may well reduce the total distance. It is likely these will prove more interesting — though you will have to use your judgement about the surrounding landscape; they will probably be a lot slower in overall travel time. On weekends and national holidays the ordinary main roads can become fearsomely congested, and you may make better time, or take the same time with more enjoyment, by sticking to the secondaries. We have proved this in summer weekends, travelling from Frinton to Hertfordshire — and on one occasion we saved ourselves immense frustration through a large slice of France on July 14th weekend, when everyone in the country decides it is time to make a move to somewhere else, with the result that there is a lot of non-movement as the arteries become choked.

Despite all the information and the clues laid before one in the average road map, there are also the false clues to make the game more difficult. Continuing to look at the map of France before me, I note that many of the D roads snake their way through various areas which I know from experience are not hilly enough to justify the squiggles. I can only conclude that they followed the boundaries of baronial estates in medieval times, and have not been important enough to reroute since. But even here there is conflicting evidence about the nature of the landscape as other nearby roads are indicated as being nearly straight. Or, from its location, related to a large river, the winding road may run adjacent to a tributory which is too minor to indicate on the map.

Map reading calls for critical analysis combined with an inquiring mind, which will not be content with quick impressions. One can still be misled over individual miles because some vital piece of information has been omitted by the cartographers, but in the main you can glean a reasonably accurate impression of what you will find in each hourly sector. Maps make fascinating reading once you have acquired the knack and entered into the spirit of this picture building game.

It will be clear, I hope, that the map which is ideal for the overall planning of a tour lasting two or three weeks, will fall sadly short of detail about those small areas one has selected as being the most rewarding for short journeys and long hours of close exploration. A solution to this problem may often be found at the local filling station, many of which sell cheap, large scale maps of the immediate area. It is always worth enquiring.

Naturally I have not attempted here anything like a comprehensive treatise on map reading. Whole manuals have been devoted to that one subject. I hope I have managed to give one or two useful tips. And that I have indicated the many hours of winter evening time that can be devoted to endless study of maps, with vast imaginative enjoyment in itself, and an altogether more successful tour as a bonus.

PUBLICATIONS, MAPS, PHRASE BOOKS

The more you know about a country you are visiting, its history, its development and topography, the more are you likely to gain from your journey. You are almost certain to find travel books for most countries in your public library.

In the course of recent researches I have been staggered by the number of specialised guide books, camp site guides, hotel guides and phrase books that have been published and are still current. Since I have not had the time to devote more than a cursory glance at only some of them, I feel I am not qualified to produce a list of recommendations. They all cost money and there is a limit to which most people can rise. Also books take up space and weigh a lot, which imposes a limit on those you can take on a motorcycle.

For the ardent camper who is going to travel widely, the AA lists all the principal camping sites in Western Europe in one publication. Again, this may not be the only one and you might do better in selecting others that deal with a single country.

The RAC and AA can supply a large range of maps. Also their Continental Handbooks are full of useful information but are bulky and slightly pricey, a substantial proportion of the text being devoted to hotels and advertisements. Their maps and publications can be supplied by post and are sold direct at their main regional offices.

The National Trust offices are usually obliging in supplying free literature of their main touring areas and other, often very useful, information if you call in or write.

In London — I advocate a visit to Stanfords, 12/14 Long Acre. (Adjacent to Covent Garden, where you can park a bike if you look round for where the others are parked). Take plenty of money if you are bitten by the travel bug. Not only are they the World's largest retailer of maps but carry phrase books and other useful travel aids and information. A friendly place, where you can browse without being pressurised.

RECOMMENDED MAPS

UK — Shell Road Maps. Approx. 3 miles to 1 inch. Excellent.
France and other countries in Europe: Michelin, Hallwag.
USA — Rand McNally.

4 Travelling in company

There is certainly no other means of surface transport where you can feel more alone and isolated than astride a motorcycle. It is, in fact, the perfect vehicle for the deep introvert. Humans, however, are basically herd animals and therefore gregarious and I most certainly belong to this group. On the other hand I have undertaken some very long journeys on my own and if one is involved in a test or journalistic mission there is the advantage that there is no one else to consider and one can press on regardless. On such occasions I have been perfectly happy with my own thoughts, and some of my most profitable and original thoughts have been developed on these solitary missions. Conversely, the adventures and the pleasures are reduced to small proportions by not being shared and I particularly miss the company during halts and at the end of the day. In my view a pleasure tour is an unmemorable event if undertaken without companionship.

THE COUPLE

Fortunately there is a convention in our society, which also satisfies certain urges, that people team up in pairs of opposite sexes. All too often after the union has been sanctified, one of the parties finds out that his/her enthusiasm for motorcycles is not shared. Although equality is now a matter of law it has not yet brought about an identity in physique, which is just as well. The male by his nature and build is the one to whom the motorcycle has the greater appeal and I will risk prosecution by averring that it is mainly females who baulk at the idea of being perched on one of those things which can cause havoc to makeup on a rainy day.

People close their ears to advice during a wooing — logic seldom prevails, but it is vital that one should break it to one's beloved that love must be shared with a two wheeled monster. It will pay to be honest — to break her in to sharing the rear half of the seat before rashly investing in a ring. Remember too, that the Sex Equality Act will not prevent her from wanting to be cherished and one should not need reminding that she is of the weaker sex. This is true in a muscular sense but when it comes to durability it is often the female that excels. Frequent will be the occasion when the fellow must be helped from the seat at the end of an exhausting day and moans while he tries to straighten up his back while dear wife is disconcertingly frisky and full of the demands of Spring. In seriousness, a shared motorcycle can be the making or breaking of a partnership, although generally adventures and hardships shared will do more to weld together than break asunder, particularly if accompanied with humour and a sense of the ridiculous.

On balance, I consider that spending a chilled and hungry night on a sodden campsite is a lot less likely to lead to friction than who should get up and make the tea during a compulsive television programme.

When a couple is contemplating a tour, it is desirable that the planning is shared, which means that the successes and the disasters are a joint responsibility without any "I told you so", either thought or spoken aloud. Even if one alone takes the initiative, it should be discussed and the democractic processes adhered to although — have you thought of it? — there can be no such thing as democracy between two people and only a tossed coin can cast the deciding vote. And let responsibility on the road be shared too, with the passenger (usually the lady), doing the route finding from a map or card which can be promptly available when required. The problem of communication between helmsman and back seat pilot is now solved, it would seem, by a simple speaking tube accessory which is now available. I have not tried this myself, but from the earliest days when a chariot was hitched on to the bike, I provided one-way communication from the sidecar via an electrically operated micro-

Two motorcyclists follow at safe distance the car in front, when entering one of the many bends of the St. Gothard pass

phone to a small ear piece in my helmet. This not only enabled Mollie to be an effective navigator — it helped her to raise both our spirits in the sloshing rain with suitable songs such as "Oh! What a beautiful morning — Oh! What a beautiful day".

Yet how many people are of the stuff of which heroes are made? Mollie perhaps, unless she was bluffing me, but I must confess that I felt inadequate and lonely at times on our various adventures and would have welcomed the support of an additional couple. Apart from sharing the problems, the exchange of ideas and impressions between two couples provide the stimulus for an enlarged appreciation.

THE SMALL GROUP

Two bikes on the road, mounted tandem or singly, can progress efficiently; three should be no problem either but remember that the progress of the group is finally determined by the man at the rear end. Four can sometimes be one too many and five becomes a convoy. The progress of six machines in a line will be erratic, as the leader slows for tail-end Charlie to catch up each time, after being separated by other vehicles or traffic lights. It is dangerous too, as there will be a tendency to bunch-up to avoid this separation. With six, the sensible thing to do is to divide into two separate groups.

So far I have merely touched on the problems of group progress and of far more importance is that of compatability. Where you have five bikes they bear five lots of people, all of whom are cussedly different. There is unlikely to be any conflict during a long weekend, one's tolerance is not strained and there is always the comforting thought that home is within one day's riding distance and it is no disaster if plans don't work out. It is a very different matter if the tour represents an annual holiday, when companionships can become unstuck at the first serious setback. For example, let us start off with a rather grim set of circumstances which, believe me, can arise.

One of the original Partitours lines up in Paris. The year is 1952 and hardly a helmet in sight

The party, mounted on five bikes, has had a dismal first day out in Northern France and have failed to achieve their target of reaching more interesting countryside. The setback starts when it rains and the picnic lunch is a washout. One bike goes down with a thump when it bumps another at a traffic light. The party becomes separated at a junction and time is lost before they reform. The nightstop proves to be an unfortunate choice and the management of the establishment is unfriendly. They wake up to more rain and a remorseless sky. Bill has a sprained ankle and sore elbow, one lady passenger has "the curse", Harry's boots are sodden, Charlie has twinges in his tummy.

Now, how is our party going to react? Ideally, morale will remain high, they will bolster each other up and accept that their own discomforts are minor, the weather temporary and they'll make an early start regardless. Yet those very same people, where they have not "gelled" will now be thinking the whole idea a bad joke. They will act indecisively and waste the whole morning in their unhappy surroundings. At this very early stage the group could split up, or even worse, friendships will dissolve and relationships for the rest of the tour will be soured. Why have things gone wrong?

In the course of our extended travels it was inevitable that Mollie and I made acquaintanceships with quite a number of small groups at hotels or campsites or when we have deliberately stopped to chat to them at the roadside. Some of these were obvious successes but the majority, from our observations, were not getting along at all happily. Rather than dwell on the negative it will probably be more constructive if I illustrate what is required to produce a compatible group. In the first place there will be unanimity about where they are going on a particular day, they will have between them at least one reasonable road map of the country and each member will have an itinerary card for that section of the journey. Elementary? You'd be surprised — or put it another way: the party that is properly organised with its routing is probably well organised in most other ways. And they will have a leader of sorts who will say "We've a lot of miles to cover yet, don't you think it is time we got

The harbour at Monte Carlo and a chosen meeting place for the first *Motorcyclist Illustrated* Monte Carlo Rally

moving? Come on Eddy, or are you going to need a helping hand?" then mutters "Why is it the smallest blokes always seem to have the heaviest bikes?"

It is probably too much to rely on having a born leader — there are not enough of them to cover every small gathering. What is needed is a mutual recognition that a coxswain is essential for team co-ordination, when the best man for the job should soon become apparent.

A party of friends or associates ought to find real enjoyment in sharing an adventure together and it is a shame when hopes are shattered along with friendships. So much depends on advance homework, the formulation of rules and procedures and the discipline to follow them through. Having had experience in planning I might prevent some anguish by outlining some of the many aspects which deserve consideration.

The incident of one bike ramming the other should not have occurred if a drill for correct spacing had been laid down and adhered to. Nor should the party have become separated at a junction, I grant that it is confusing on the Continent, where alternative routes are signed as you go into their towns, one being compulsory for heavy vehicles, which is sometimes the quicker road, the other being optional for cars. This separation was the fault of the leader who, in lieu of having eyes in the back of his head, must use his mirrors, and ensure that his 'tail' is in view before he proceeds at an intersection where there might be confusion. If a party is split in two at a traffic light, all the members of the first half should have anticipated that this could happen, and wait for the others at the other side of the crossing or, depending on circumstances, proceed very slowly until contact is re-established.

The tail end must be confident about this, to prevent them riding too close or taking a risk by rushing a light. Rules of the road are the most important of all and it is a collective responsibility that the laws and customs of the countries they are visiting should be understood. It must also be remembered that on the open road if one stops, you all stop and if five people do it individually for five minutes in every hour, your average touring speed is cut by nearly one half. The habitual running-low-on-fuel fellow is a menace. Fill to the brim at night if there is a convenient place nearby and at intermediary re-fills you should all do so together and check your oil and luggage and what-have-you at the same time. If one person starts to feel uncomfortable five minutes after leaving a well-appointed filling station and has to stop for a roadside bush, it is an indication of poor bladder control or improvidence, and the culprit deserves to be chided.

The same thing applies to machine maintenance and attaching luggage prior to starting off in the morning; the time of departure rests on the last one. Method and co-ordination might have to be evolved through experience but a few rules at the start will emphasise the need and rules can always be added to or modified. The little things, like parking your machines at the same angle from the kerb and equidistant from each other makes for mutual convenience. Does this sound like regimentation? Well, there is only one alternative to order and that is disorder which, in this case, means that bikes are parked higgledy piggledy, taking up more space than need be, and when one fellow wants to take something out of his luggage he has to perform contortions and perhaps tip someone else's bike off its prop stand.

Brief refreshment stops are desirable on a long run but will play havoc with a schedule. At the mid-morning or afternoon brew up, there should be no delays in taking out stoves, kettles, water. There is little advantage to every person acting independently as this will result in a lot of unpacking by members operating at different speeds. There is bound to be one fellow, such as myself, who stows his water container in a different place to his stove with a perfectly logical reason but fails to remember the logic when the time comes to assemble all requirements. If there is a certain amount of sharing out the preparations in a methodical way it can be a great time saver.

I am afflicted by invisible 'borrowers', I have only to put a thing down to have it removed to somewhere else the moment my back is turned. Consequently I am a disorganised picnicker or camper left to my own devices, although I become an entirely efficient member of a team.

As already mentioned, it is essential that each member should know the route he is following, the easiest way is to prepare a route card at the morning briefing, so that all are agreed. Where there is no pre-determined night stop, it is also vital to agree to a meeting point for the latter part of the day. Outside a main Post Office of a particular town is a sensible-choice, and do not think this precaution is unimportant, as people can still become separated, even in the best regulated families. We once met a fellow on a BMW in the Italian Alps, who had lost contact with his partner the day before and was at a loss about what to do. I have no idea if he became re-united. Quite possibly not.

Not everyone is equally prosperous (or poor). A daily budget for all must be agreed upon from the beginning — this will control the frequency and price of restaurant meals and night stops. If one rider has to work within a close margin he may well find that frequent cafe stops for refreshment are more than he can afford. All these little details call for decisions and rules. I will pass on one helpful rule we established on our Partitours — 'No treating'. This means you buy your own as and when you wish, without embarrassment or misunderstanding, and if one person does treat another it is understood that he does not expect to be treated back. Actually, this is a Continental custom of which I approve. If I treat someone to a drink, or whatever, then let it be my gesture, which is not so if it is only my turn. Our 'No treat' rule works fine — you can be poor quietly on your own, without it showing, and if you're a one drink man, that's better than being a roundsman when you are in charge of a vehicle.

In my view it is not the individual constituents of a group which makes for success or failure so much as having well worked out plans and rules and conforming to them and this leads me straight away to:

ORGANISED TOURS

Unquestionably the least complicated and least worrisome way of making a first tour abroad is to join a group which is expertly arranged by experienced people.

The first name that springs to mind is the International Motorcyclists Tour Club — known, for short, as the IMTC and in 1976 there was a newcomer in the field, *Motor Cyclist Illustrated,* which arranged the first Monte Carlo Rally for motorcycles and proposes to run additional Rallies in future years. I participated in the Monte Carlo which was, in effect, an organised tour, although it lasted for only seven days (six nights) and involved long

Morning preparation for the day's ride in mid-France. The Honda in the forefront is a spectator only

runs and tight schedules. The tour included a travelling mechanic and a float to collect the machine casualties. The run involved too much motorway for my liking but it was intended to appeal to folk with Superbikes, who wanted the chance to give them a long distance airing. I certainly do not wish to sound contemptuous, because I thoroughly enjoyed it too, both the company and complete freedom from worry or responsibility.

I am led to believe that the IMTC Partitours operate rather as ours used to and accordingly I will take ours as the example.

It was Mollie and I who organised the first post-war group tour in 1949 — the IMTC ran a number before the war — and ours were also called Partitours. It was not that we intended to borrow the name, it just happened that way when the first editorial announcement appeared in the *Motor Cycle* and the name stuck. In all we ran about 40 tours, the last one being in 1969.

Organised tours usually comprise 25 motorcycles and upwards, which split up into groups of from two to five on the road, the groups becoming widely separated in time and distance during each day's scheduled run. In general, travelling companions have sorted themselves out by the start of the second day into compatible little groups that stay together for the rest of the tour. In fact, there are rarely problems of incompatability or friction on a large tour. If the organisers have done their job there will be rules and procedures for all probable contingencies, which have been discussed with the assembled party as well as supplied in written form. For the benefit of other organisers and participants, existing and potential, and posterity in general, I reckon I should have something useful to impart and I will outline a few of the main features of our past operations. First of all I must make it clear that ours were not run commercially, the reward for our work being our interest in the game, although we expected the bulk of our own costs to be covered. Our publicity consisted only of free, editorial announcements in the motorcycling journals, and in response to inquiries we sent duplicated information — no pictures, no frills — about the date, destination and approximate cost of the proposed tours. We spent countless days during the winter months brooding over maps, to select a varied and interesting route and, since every hotel

Chalon-sur-Soane and the night's stop, on the way down to Monte Carlo

was pre-booked, each day's run had to be a practicable proposition regardless of the weather. It is a major problem to plan an unalterable daily mileage in advance. For mountain stretches, there would be the need to supply alternative low and high routings. It is no joy coping with high passes in fog or sleet and there is also the possibility of a pass being closed by snow, even in high summer.

One ruling was that groups on the road should never exceed five machines but, on the other hand, no rider should ever set out on his own. A single lost person, without a companion, who fails to turn up at night is a dire worry to organisers — infinitely more than a group who, presumably will not all have perished over the same precipice! Despite all precautions, we have lost contact with people for more than a day and we have been powerless except to notify the police, who have nearly always been amazingly co-operative in different countries, including widespread broadcasting over their radio. Happily, all the 1,400 or so participants over the years have all been accounted for, but there have been anxious moments. There was even one fellow who picked up a Swiss female passenger and made off to Switzerland for the rest of the tour, who did not think to notify us! One cannot account for people, not all of them, but this was the worst case of irresponsible behaviour.

If only more women would convince themselves that they too can ride big bikes and enjoy it

John and Liz McDermott stamp Ken Craven's route card on his arrival at the finishing point of the 1976 Monte Carlo Rally

The rider of this Silk two-stroke twin carried all his requirements for the Monte Carlo Rally within his single tank bag

A cover takes up precious little space yet can prove useful for protecting the machine, when parked

A mute admission that the standard Kawasaki seat gets a little hard when riding long distances

Picnicking is the best method—it's also the cheapest

On another occasion we lost one fellow on the last three days of the tour and he never did catch up with us. He knowingly broke all the rules by not waiting for his group, setting off on his own early in the morning, having left his route itinerary and hotel list in his room. We tracked him down through the British Consulate in Paris (he had approached the Consul in Barcelona, a city where he should not have been) and we had a strip torn off us for having abandoned a member of our party! Then his parents threatened to take us to court for compensation! We had used foresight — and let this be a warning to others who bear responsibility for groups, no matter how large or small. This is a harsh world where not everyone behaves with a sense of decency, so it is vital that all participants must sign a declaration that they will not hold the organisation responsible for the consequences of accidents or misadventure and a whole lot of other potential misfortunes besides. We had taken legal advice from a friend about the wording of the undertaking which, however, also included our obligations.

Our main obligations were the booking of hotels and ensuring they were paid (substantially by advanced draft), the detailed preparation of the route and the issuing of tickets for the Channel ferry crossing (although members were free to arrange their own if they preferred) and then to ensure that all the final lists and tickets were despatched in good time, by registered post.

Of particular importance to ensure the success of a tour was the weekend get-together a few weeks before setting out. Most participants managed to attend, even though many had to travel hundreds of miles in each direction for the event. These occasions were rehearsals, where folk came to know each other and most of the small groupings were established at that time. Here we could discuss the rules, regulations and procedures, so that they not only knew them but fully accepted the logic behind them. Then, on the quiet, I would wander round inspecting the array of machinery, on the lookout for worn tyres and sad chains and overall condition, so that I could later raise the matter with the owner, if need be. If I spotted a real old heap, and it happened a few times, as not all folk interpret regulations the same way, I would then approach the owner and feign assumption that this was his daily go-to-work hack and not the one he was proposing to use on the tour itself. More than once we had to disqualify people because their mounts were not in suitable condition, which might not only give them trouble but their companions as well. Let us be clear, there was no regimentation of our parties. We used our authority only over important issues that were for the mutual good. In fact, from the start we tried to convey to applicants they were not just fare-paying passengers but participants in a joint adventure and we invited comment on various aspects. Mollie was the accepted leader, chairman and organising secretary, while I was merely her

Nothing more need be said—these two are so obviously enjoying themselves upon their Norton Dominator in the Dolomites

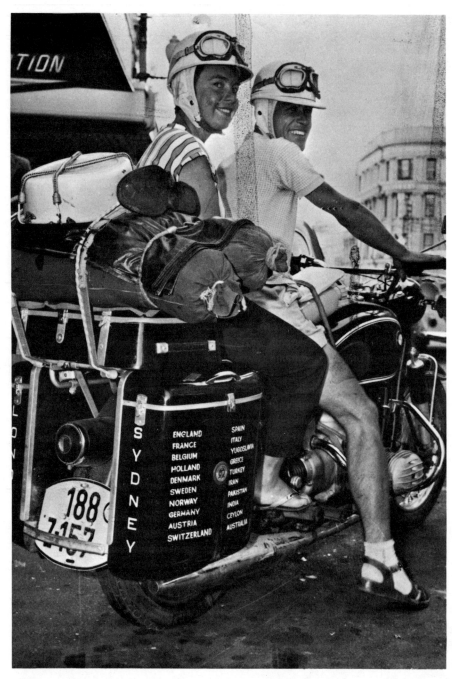

John Galvin on his way back to Australia with his new wife. Note the stops listed on the pannier side

assistant. Continentals are prone to being less enlightened about the role of women and the waiters and other diners always seemed mildly surprised when the assembled party would relapse into silence when she tapped on a plate. Probably the only regimental ruling was that all should be packed and ready for breakfast at an appointed hour. This made sense, too, as this was the best time for reviewing the route for the day and for sorting out possible problems such as:

"Harry, he's experiencing some mag. trouble. Is there a wizard with electrics among us who could lend him a hand and has anyone a spare set of points?"

With large parties it is inevitable that over the years there would be more serious accidents or incidents of some sort, yet there was the understanding that the responsibility of the leaders was to the group as a whole and they should not be so delayed that they could not reach the scheduled destination by the same night. How did we cope? It was a great help that we had a lot of 'regulars' on our tours who became our able lieutenants but even without these there is a great team spirit among motorcyclists and most can be relied on to help even at some sacrifice to themselves. Every calamity poses different problems which must be dealt with according to circumstances.

An unusual view of a very recent Partitour, obviously in a hot clime

In the event of serious mechanical trouble or accident damage, if the bikes were theoretically repairable on the spot within a day or two, then repaired they were. In these instances a couple of members with the right qualifications could always be found in the party who would volunteer to cope with the trouble and catch us up either at the halfway point, where we would stay for two or three days, or cut across the return loop. Thus, with the aid of a local repair shop or just a village blacksmith, some remarkable repairs were carried out. These included bent forks, broken frames and even an engine which had had a piece knocked out of its crankcase due to sharp contact with a roadside boulder.

There have been injuries also, though remarkably only three cases requiring hospitalisation for more than a couple of days. The most serious of these was a fractured skull, which rendered the victim unconscious for several days although happily he survived without permanent brain damage. We only learned about the accident when we arrived at our hotel that night, which happened to be within 20 miles of the hospital where he had been taken. Naturally, we had a list of addresses and phone numbers to contact for all our party and we telephoned the parents, who were able to fly out the next day. The rest of his group gallantly volunteered to stand by until their arrival, after Mollie and I had dealt with police enquiries. As anticipated, the group caught us up by the early hours of the morning to find that a cold supper, wine and a thermos flask of coffee had been set out for them. These little details have to be thought of and arranged regardless of distracting circumstances and our lieutenants were schooled to act on our behalf if we happened to be detained. This brings me to the point that leaders must make provision for the tour to carry on without them. We escaped certain death by inches and a miracle (in consequence of my own bad judgement) on the second day out of our first Partitour and thereafter we did not assume we were born to be immortal, or more cheerfully, that we would never be forced to drop out. This never happened but there were two occasions when we fell behind by a day and the party carried on smoothly.

Another Partitour institution was the 'whipround' when we would ask all participants to contribute a specific amount to offset exceptional expenses incurred by one of the party when only financial help would enable him to carry on. This was a valuable mutual insurance and to save embarrassment by the recipient and resentment among the donors, the scheme was outlined in our circulars and administered by a small committee when the need arose. This did not obviate the need for individual insurance with commercial companies, but was a supplement to it, particularly as they do not pay cash on the spot.

A number of our tours were unique without a present day counterpart. These were the specially tough ones to the back and beyond, which were arranged every third or fourth year at the request of our veterans. They were dubbed 'The Craven International Seventeen Day Trials' and metal commemorative badges for the machines were produced for participants. One of these tours used minor roads in inland Yugoslavia, another followed the worst section of the Liege-Sofia-Liege Rally, which at that time was about the toughest European event for automobiles. Tackling this road was akin to going round Cape Horn on a Square rigger! I reckon the idea could be revised and get a good deal of support. Who will do it? It would now be more difficult to find suitably difficult through routes — as apart from dead end tracks — although there is still a minor network from central Spain to the Mediterranean which would prove trying to modern motorcycles less suited to coping with the rough than the old British bangers.

Many of the older, more sophisticated types, approached the idea of joining our groups with considerable reserve and caution and it could take some persuading before they would make up their minds. They need not have worried, our groups were made up of all types from the young semi-skilled to doctors and others in the professions. This was true of the Monte Carlo and it is my impression this is so with other organised groups. And they all mix well too, on a motorcycle one becomes classless. Nor are they organised just for first timers abroad. If you have been a lot of places on your own, try a party for a change. They are both very different and hard to compare, but a well organised group tour should be a cheerful and unforgettable experience.

5 Camping and camp cooking

LIBERATOR AND MONEY STRETCHER

There is nothing like travelling by motorcycle to give one a sense of freedom, of escape from the bonds and ties of the world. It is only towards the end of the day, as one searches for a roof for the night, that one realises the extent of one's dependence on others, and that freedom is a very transitory thing, particularly so if you are only one of many who is looking for a friendly place at a reasonable price. Available accommodation on holiday routes and vacation areas has not kept pace with the increase in motorised tourism. It was the need rather than the inclination that brought me back to camping after the lapse of a great many years. In fact, it was only for the first few summers after the war when we took with us the most rudimentary equipment for spending a night out; a course which we took unwillingly and only in the most favourable circumstances or when we could not find a room which came within our meagre budget.

Now that I am better equipped and possess more know-how, I have become a positive convert, which is more than being virtually assured of a place to erect one's own roof at most times to suit one's inclination. This is an important extension of the freedom of travel. The saving too is a delight. My conversion to camping, however, has greater depths than the practical considerations alone. I find there is something satisfying and adventurous in creating one's own little igloo from such little material. There's more to it still — camping folk, whether in mini-tents or luxury trailer caravans, are in the main friendly and for the time being classless. Put those same identical neighbours from the camp site into an hotel dining room and they become non-communicating individuals or self-contained family groups.

To deal specifically with the motorcycling aspect first, there are campers who use motorcycles, their main habitat being the USA, although a similar but lesser breed emanate from Germany. This group take their camping seriously and require a large tent complete with hanging lamp, sumptous bed roll and such amenities as the kitchen sink (plastic version). If their needs cannot be piled on the motorcycle they expand to a two wheel trailer, a wide selection being marketed that includes a massive version which expands upwards, to become a caravan.

Forgive me, Americans, I am not being in the slightest contemptuous. Yours is a very big country and I can see the attraction of pitching one's home in a wonderful forest of lakes and rivers, by the foothills of mountains or on the fringe of a fascinating desert, and using it as base for day-long excursions with the unemcumbered mount. Different places make for differing customs.

I belong, however, to another breed of camping motorcyclist, the emphasis being on the motorcycling — a restless type always wanting to be on the move and free of excessive encumbrance. To me the basic requirements are a small crawl-in-tent which is just adequate for two (assuming one is sharing) with ground sheet, inflatable lilos and bedding. I have deliberately not been specific about the bedding as this is a matter of choice. I have found the lightweight zip-up quilted variety to be effective if weighted down with one's rainkit and outer clothing but, being of a slithery material, anything placed on top tends to work its way off and one finds oneself groping madly for the lost covering in the chill hours of night. Also they are the very devil to compress into an acceptably small bundle: they fight back and it is rather like trying to squeeze a toy balloon into a small basin — though why one should want to do this is another matter. My preference for the two of us is a couple of old woollen blankets which, for solo occupation, can be sewn round the edges to form an envelope, not forgetting to

leave a narrow end open for entry. Again, one piles on one's surplus and discarded garments for warmth, and there is a fair chance they will stay put if you are not a restless sleeper.

Flying things that bite are the bane of the camper and it is no luxury to carry a small aerosol to spray out the tent shortly before you enter for the night. I advocate the use of mesh to cover tent apertures (some tents are so equipped when bought). This will not exclude a few of the most persistent mosquitoes — actually the tent then becomes a trap and you can have the satisfaction of shooting down the marauders, taking cover under the blanket until the air clears.

The camping and cooking utensils for two — little more is involved than for one — will still occupy a lot of available luggage space and by available I mean panniers and top case — or, lacking a top case, a neat and modest mound. This calls for restraint in the selection of garments, to leave enough area for the camping paraphernalia The tough and confirmed camper is not in need of finery and for him it is less of a problem than for folk like me, for (let me whisper) I am a Sybarite who enjoys the occasional night at a hotel — most particularly when it is raining!

CAMP SITES

In Britain and most of the rest of Europe one is seldom more than a half hour's ride away from a camp site. Sometimes you will pass them every few minutes, although I can think of some areas, such as inland Spain, where you will be lucky to find one at all. The variety and amenities provided in camps range from the primitively simple, with earth closets and a supply of cold water, to the lavishly equipped, with hot showers and a food and provision store. There are many which are really holiday camps which aim to appeal to long-stay visitors and which have restaurants, swimming pool and even boating lakes.

I regard a camp site publication as a **must** for all the countries through which one travels and I say this even though I seldom end up at a site I have pre-selected. The reason for this is that I may spot the perfect site before I reach my selection or I may be in the mood to push on a lot more miles, when it helps to know there is a choice. Alternatively, I may reject them, because I don't like the look of the place. However accurately the camping guides may describe a place — the services and amenities are shown in symbols and there will be an indication about its location, whether it is rural or has outstanding views — it is much more difficult to convey its atmosphere. For the motorcyclist, more often than not, the sites that have everything are the least appealing, even though they may be perfect for the motor drawn caravans.

When I look back on the best sites I have known, they do not conform to any one category. I can think of an **au ferme** (on the farm) in France which offers simply a field with a few trees and only basic amenities. Yet it has charm and here ones' neighbours are the nicest people for, whatever they may be in their other lives, the cordiality of the farmer brings out the best in everyone. At the top end of the scale is a de luxe establishment, swimming pool and all, on the outskirts of Benidorm (of all places) which is set down in palms and orange groves. The worst I have seen is also in Spain, from which I promptly turned away. This too had all the luxuries but it was one immense sprawling suburbia of every shape and size of tent and all varieties of homes on wheels.

You may not always be able to find the place you want but as a camper you can be sure as you will ever be in this uncertain world that you will find somewhere to lay your weary head. From the poor to the superlative, and all that lie in between, they all manage somehow to be so different that each night is a fresh adventure. I think I can recall at least on detail of every one of the places I have camped out — I'm blessed if I can do the same with hotels.

OFF SITE CAMPING

Purists may well maintain that camping on even the most austere camping site is not camping in the true sense, but in most of Europe you are not free to park your tent along the highway or on common land at whim without the likelihood you are breaking some bye-law. In some countries, notably Yugoslavia which is a popular touring area, it is strictly against the law and doing so is likely to involve you in a tedious session with the police, which will end with a fine. In most other countries they are not quite so fussy, although there is the prospect of being moved on at a possibly awkward time. On the other hand, Yugoslavia apart, I doubt if objection will be raised on mountain slopes and remoter uncultivated regions, my only advice here being to pull out of sight of the road and cause no damage. What the police do not see the law will not grieve, and they are not likely to care, if it is done with discretion. I have met Americans who have 'done' a large slice of Europe while hardly ever using a camping site and, may be through ignorance, possibly through cunning, they have experienced no problem. For my part, I am nervous about camping in the wilds for I instinctively recall instances of dreadful happenings to travellers. This is very cowardly of me as the prospect of being murdered by marauding villains is rather less than being struck by lightning. On the other hand I am not very happy about nearby lightning either when exposed on a motorcycle!

The premise, as always, is that the touring motorcyclist who intends to camp, and cook his own meals, has very little space into which to pack the utensils and foodstuffs which, at home, spread themselves round an entire kitchen. And even the smallest of these, in a micro-batchelor-flat, provides more room than part of one pannier case! All too often, the situation results in the camper having a sausage-bacon-egg or bean fry-up which, however acceptable in itself, becomes tedious when repeated twice daily for three weeks. It can also have an unfortunate effect on the digestion....

The problem, and its solution, divides itself into three sections: what utensils to take; what foodstuffs to bring and what to purchase locally; and what menus can be thought of which are practicable with such limited resources, yet offer gastronomic variety and nutritional balance.

Starting with the utensils, the principle is that every item taken should be capable of a double purpose. Thus a plastic cup may seem an attractive idea: it is light, and often squashable and unbreakable to within wide limits. But what can be done with it? It is a container, from which liquids can be imbibed ranging from soft drinks via tea or coffee to soups. And that is all. By contrast, a metal mug can be put over an open flame, or on top of the lid of another covered vessel being used for cooking. Tea can be made in it as well as drunk from it: in one small item are combined the facilities of kettle, teapot and cup! It has the snag for the unwary that the first eager sip of a long-awaited cuppa results in a scorched lip, but the lesson is quickly learned (very!) so this is as nothing compared with the advantages. And I haven't finished with these yet. Instant potatoes can be made in it, sauces kept hot while the dish they are to garnish is being cooked, and so on, for as far as the imagination can stretch.

The basic tool is the stove, which lends itself to the separate descriptions, but does not need illustrating. Next comes the cooking pan, about which I have strong views, based on wide experience of the right kind, and seeing others struggling hopefully but helplessly with the wrong. It should be a heavy base, deep frying pan, preferably of the skillet type: that is, with two small loop handles, on which admittedly it is all too easy to scorch one's fingers, but which assist stowing securely on top of rain gear or other loose luggage. A long handle here can be a nuisance; it is also difficult to balance on the small camping stove, but all too easy to knock off. My preference is for the cast iron, unlined variety, but in these days of wear-it-out then throw-it-away substitutes for the sound and durable, I am at a loss to suggest where the ideal might be obtainable. When faced at your local store with a wide variety, each of which on closer inspection turns out to be fundamentally the same, one can but keep in mind the reason for the choice and select what most closely approximates to it. Small camp stoves concentrate the flame over a small area. A heavy base spreads the heat; that popular type of rectangular pan with fold-over handle doesn't, and therefore is the main cause of those culinary catastrophes associated with camp cooking. Mollie and I have tried an asbestos pad in conjunction with a lightweight pan, but without success: they are over-effective and disperse most of the heat to the outside. Furthermore, they soon become brittle with use and they are not easy things to stow without flexing, when obviously they break up.

Next comes two plates large enough to cover the main pan. One of these does more than provide a lid when such is called for by the nature of the cooking; it also becomes a hot-plate. The chef can then prepare two items which require to be separated, the one being cooked in the skillet while the other, previously done, is kept hot above — either simply on one plate or sandwiched between the two, according to its nature. This rescues the chef from having to say to his companion: "Which do you prefer, a hot dish and cold sauce, or hot sauce and cold dish: I can't do both on the one ring". With this system he can! What's more, the hot meal will then be eaten off hot plates.

Two half-pint mugs have already been indicated: and desirably these items should be of metal, finished in vitreous enamel. Yes, I know the enamel can flake off if carelessly thumped against another hard object, but overall they are durable and the occasional flaked-away bit does not greatly detract from their utility. The enamel also offers modest but significant protection to sensitive lips when a mug is used for a hot drink. When a mug is used to cook soup, incidentally, or similar liquid, more continuous stirring may well be necessary to avoid scorching than with the more conventional utensil. I also commend an enamelled metal teapot, despite what I have said about the brew up potential of the mugs. A kettle will be required, and the metal teapot will serve this purpose as well.

To summarise, we now have a frying pan, teapot, two mugs and two plates, (and by subsidiary use, also a stewing pan with optional lid, kettle, two small saucepans, two mixing basins, two soup bowls and a hot-plate)

The nearly old and the nearly new. Provided the machine is in first class condition its age is not important

giving an adequate range of cooking and eating utensils reduced to a happy minimum from the point of view of the motorcycle's carrying capacity. Making the best use of them is a matter of mental agility and manual dexterity. So you mix the instant mash in one of the mugs which is wanted immediately afterwards for the brew. Now is the time to find there is no water available for rinsing it out. Husband dashes to the water tap at the other side of the camping pitch, colliding with two infants which have just run out from a nearby caravan. Oh yes! the hitches are innumerable and, since we are human, one has to exhaust all the dire mistakes by personally making them. The trouble is that the permutations seem limitless and I have only touched on a few of them: but that applies to most things in life.

So much for the means: now for the food, the first question being what to take, what to obtain on the journey. It is, I assert, a universally held belief by the average insular Britisher, that the substances foreigners use will be unfit for human British cooking and that therefore, the only possible thing to do is to bring with one enough to provide for every meal throughout the trip. This view is not strictly accurate. Indeed, it is more than possible that a considerable proportion of that same Britisher's normal diet was grown in the countries he now intends to visit, and was imported. Myself, I like to take English jams and marmalade, English tea (the brands of tea widely **sold** in England) and bacon.

Personal preferences of this nature apart, the two questions worthy of consideration are of quantities and prices. Take salt, for example. If this is left to be purchased en route, the minimum quantity sold would prove sufficient for months of normal consumption, resulting in valuable packing space being lost. Sugar is sold in one-kilo lots, and there will be those for whom this is too much; in which case they should consider taking a smaller quantity with them. Similarly, with all other condiments, spices and the like. The crucial question is only rarely one of availability, more often of quantity and packing space.

On the other hand, the idea that continental food is more costly than that available at home, is often, though not always, true. Personally, I take with me some at least of my preferred spices and herbs, salt, sugar, tea, coffee, cornflour (easier to use than flour for thickening) and powdered milk — and here I like the full cream variety. If I take butter, it is in minimal quantities, carefully packed in a safe container like a screwtop jar so that, when it melts, it will not permeate the entire pannier case and all its other contents. So too take care with all other foodstuffs. Can you imagine the disastrous concoction which would result from the free release of coffee, sugar and oily substances? I don't have to imagine: I have experienced it!

If my advice is followed and a big-mileage is planned for the first day, there is merit also in having selected at home foodstuffs which will permit adequate eating on that day with the least possible effort: say, a tin of a favoured meaty dish, or a simple-to-prepare meal of the kind sold in packets, which requires only cooking in a quantity of boiling water. Indeed, it is a good idea to ensure that there is always left available one such meal against the times when the day's end comes with only a single thought in mind: to set up camp, eat, and get to sleep with the least effort and greatest speed.

Ancillaries to take from home, may properly include detergents, either liquid or powdered, and a cloth suitable for holding hot handles or plates as well as wiping up afterwards, choosing the variety which are easy to wash out. As for packing, in addition to safety from spillage on the way, two points are worth remembering: that round containers take up more space than square ones for the same capacity and that glass is heavy to carry, and liable to break. Oh yes, and something I forgot to say about foodstuffs: condensed milk in tins. Tempting; but unless the whole contents are used in one go, how does one safely pack the remainder? If you are at all like me, you will forget many such things, on many occasions, throughout your touring life. Don't be disheartened: you are not alone!

Finally, some words about what to attempt by way of camp cooking for the bulk of the tour.

It is a fact — and I say this without condescension — that the young or younger have massive (and to me, enviable) appetites which do not require gastronomic titillation. The main requirement is food as quickly as possible from the time of staking out their site. If it is only a matter of instant spud, a tinned or packaged meal, the more delectable possibilities which I will outline are likely to be of only academic interest.

The trouble with over-simple food is that they result in an unbalanced diet. If the younger digestion can cope, the older may soon begin to protest. Mollie and I have developed quite sophisticated tastes and talents: we are both competent cooks, and fortunately both like the Mediterranean style of eating. We have therefore evolved a number of menus which can be coped with efficiently, using only the simple tools I have outlined above. These menus rely heavily on onions and tomatoes, both of which are readily available in most parts of Europe. In the south there is in particular a type of tomato, irregularly-shaped and less brilliantly coloured than the smooth, highly cultivated variety so familiar at home. They have the great merits of being widely available, crisply tasty — and very cheap! As one travels further south, the mild green or red peppers which are well known in England as a vegetable, but tend to be expensive, become cheaper with almost every mile.

Onions and tomatoes, by themselves, form the basis of many tasty meals: in the form of a flavoursome sauce. It is made by heating a small amount of fat or oil into which sliced onion is stirred round while it is fairly hot. Then put a lid on and cook slowly. When half done, add the tomatoes and cover up again. Into this sauce may be dropped, at the appropriate moment, a variety of other items giving different meals from the same essential base. Those red and green peppers I have mentioned, go in early, before the tomato. Meat requires separate cooking first, then being transferred to the 'hot-plate' above until the sauce is ready to receive it.

Pork is a favourite of mine. It is important, if the risk of infection is to be avoided, that it is cooked right through. This does not mean frying to a frazzle, but rather ensuring that every trace of pink meat has changed its colour: easy to see with sliced meat, more difficult with chops: if in doubt, slice through at the thickest part, and have a look. (You will realise, from my saying this, that I am anticipating that a camp cook who has had very little experience at home, may attempt some of these dishes: there is absolutely no reason why he should not). Brown the pork slices or chops in hot fat, then transfer them temporarily to the hot-plate above, while the sauce is being dealt with. Put the meat back when the tomatoes are added (complete with skins), and let it all steam. Don't forget the salt, will you? The result is delectable! and it cannot, by any stretch of the imagination, be called difficult. Nor does it take long: 45 minutes at most, from start to finish.

Variations are equally easy to obtain. Instant mash is a highly acceptable filler to go with the meal — and from time to time rice can be used instead. For pork read lamb or chicken, according to taste, or the desire for something different from last time. By adding minced meat to the same basic sauce, we have the garnishing for a fine spaghetti bolognaise.

Mollie and I have a particular love for salads, and there is no problem about obtaining the ingredients during the summer season. We also like garlic: don't be afraid of trying it! A salad, in addition to any of the above variations, now produces a fully balanced nutritional meal, as well as a tasty one.

There is a French saying from the eighteenth century which goes "The English have sixty religious sects but only one sauce". Perhaps the same can be said of my one contribution to more imaginative camp cooking but onions and tomatoes can be regarded only as a basis for many variations and, since their preparation is rather more involved than packaged instant nosh, it is unlikely that you will resort to it so frequently that it becomes monotonous.

Camping, at home anyway, is quite easy with the right weather and site, and is well within the bounds of both scooters and mopeds

Although I rather depricate the use of prepared meals for everyday living, the dehydrated variety concentrate a lot of nourishment in a small sachet of little weight and they are a godsend for the motorcyclist. There is an immense variety now available and there is scope for ingenuity and imagination in their selection.

Although a gastronomic insult can be very welcome, and even digested when one is famished at the end of a long day, it must be remembered that food is the source of our energy and this can decline after a number of days on a scurvy diet. Yet a high proportion of those same people who know a lot about their motorbikes, their needs and maintenance, set off in total ignorance about their own needs, for the right sort of fuel and its processing — in other words, food and its preparation. So, if you are intending to rely almost entirely on your own cooking, not restaurant meals, for the duration of a holiday tour, then surely the subject demands consideration along with all your other planning. Have a go in your own kitchen at preparing meals on one burner, using the same limited utensils and the sort of ingredients that will be available to you on a tour. With practice, one can turn out some tasty concoctions which can add variety to one's usual diet and, quite possibly, cut down on the domestic fuel bill!

Campers, with the inevitable few exceptions, conform to the code of keeping sites free of litter and generally show consideration for each other and the management of the place. I wonder if they are equally conscientious about their picnic sites, which are not self-policing? On second thoughts it is likely to be non-campers who are the culprits. Yet select any ideal picnic spot, even in remote areas, and you will almost certainly find that it has become a refuse dump. This applies in almost any country except to a large extent the USA which has now been cleaned up through the imposition of fines as high as $500 and no argument! What a comment on society!

In Corfe Castle, Dorset, there is a display cabinet containing an array of litter which has been assembled to look particularly revolting and underneath a sign which reads something like this "Objects picked up in one day within the confines of the castle. Relics of a decadent civilisation".

I go along with this and in less optimistic moods I wonder, whither humanity? Do we have to bespoil everything with which we come in contact? I think of the countless times I and my associates have had to clean up *ordure* (the descriptive French word for garbage) in self-protection, to be able to enjoy a meal and relax in hygenic surroundings. Cleaning up after one's stay is really no problem at all. Orange peel and other vegetable matter, crushed eggshells, napkins and paper, if shredded, will dissolve into humus fairly quickly, given moisture, and only need to be buried shallowly or concealed away at the root of a bush, if there is no other course. But bottles, plastic bags and containers are nigh indestructible and metal cans remain an eyesore for a year and more before they rust away. If there was space in the luggage to bring food along, there remains more space to carry away the wrappings for disposal at a convenient refuse bin. This sort of gesture may be wasted on the desert air but some of us must start by setting an example and, if nothing else, at least one's conscience remains clear.

A simple screen, such as this Stadium design, helps to reduce rider fatigue, even on a 250cc machine

6 Keeping warm and dry

In the precise and pedantic sense there is no such thing as warm clothing unless it is heated by electricity or some other outside source. All that garments can do is to retain the warmth of the human body and form a barrier against the cold outer air. This is a statement of the obvious, though it is too often overlooked, and I am using it now on which to build my theme. To continue.

Restriction of the blood circulation to any part of the body has the same result as say, slowing down the flow of hot water through a central heating system, when heat will be dissipated through radiation more quickly than it is replenished. With the body the surface temperature will drop and so will the retained heat in the garment gradually decline. Thus the first rule is the avoidance of restrictive garments. Too many layers can have the same effect, unless carefully planned in sequence, with each tier being of larger dimension than the last and ending up with a really massive outer covering. Yet even in this there lies the snag that the combined weight of the total will substantially be borne by the shoulders and so restrict circulation to the arms and hands. If the answer does not lie with weight or volume, what then?

To start with the first intimate item next to oneself, scientists and other knowledgeable folk advocate the string vest or open weave fabric, in which a pocket of warm air forms in each little open cell. But what if cold air is trapped in each little cell? I must not refute the pundits but I have never had the nerve to try open mesh underwear on Elephant Rallies or other winter events, when I am prepared for freezing temperatures. In these circumstances, I have relied on what I know and this consists of 'long johns,' one piece woollen underwear extending from the ankles to the neck and down to the wrists. I have an idea that this type of garment might be hard to find outside theatrical costumiers who cater for bedroom farces, so it's back to open weave underwear, boys and girls. But this is no help for knees and thighs. One piece tights might supply the answer; for men too — don't worry, no one need know!

Up to now I have dealt with fully enshrouding underwear, which is significant only if you are contemplating a long run through continuing Arctic conditions. It is hardly likely on a Summer tour that you will carry an emergency reserve, which would necessitate stripping right down to the buttocks when ascending a high mountain during inclement weather when, believe me, it can become mighty chilly. But if I carry on with relating how I prepared for a Winter epic it will at least give some indication of how to cope with more moderate cold.

The coldest Elephant Rally ever was in January 1963, with snow and ice throughout the journey and no daytime thaw. At night and at higher altitudes the temperature dropped below zero Fahrenheit. I was mounted on a potent Matchless 650 twin to which was hitched a Wessex sidecar — a wonderful combination — and was accompanied by Barry Ryerson, then Editor of *Motorcyclist Illustrated,* riding a Work's BSA and Watsonian sidecar. This was a press stunt which I had inaugurated which, among other things, was to test my theories about keeping warm: theories that had developed from a run the previous winter to a ski resort in Swtizerland where I did a fine job at breaking my leg when trying out these dangerous things which are clamped to the feet, lack brakes and from which you can't bale out in hopeless situations. But that is another story.

For the venture my clothes consisted of 'long johns', cotton shirt, one short sleeved and one long sleeved pullover, both lightweight wool, Harris tweed Jacket and trousers of 50% wool mixture. My outer weather kit was a two piece Barbour suit of the type made of heavyweight cotton fabric, which is proofed with a waxy

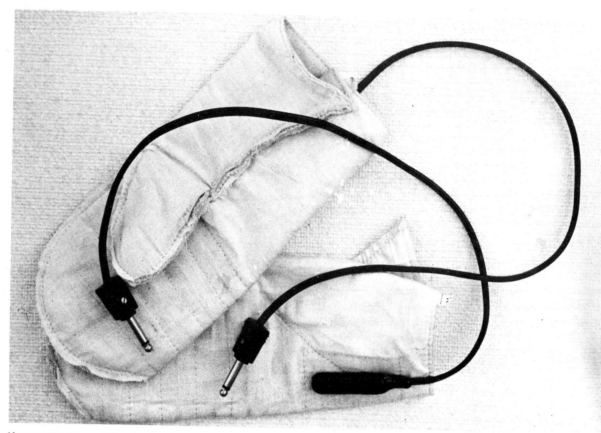

If you suffer from cold hands, electric gloves are the only real answer in very low temperatures. Over gloves have to be worn too

With a fairing of this type electrical connections are easy to locate

substance. The whole ensemble was not bulky and permitted plenty of free movement and the Barbour suit accounted for most of the weight so that there was little imposition on the shoulders. My preference for natural fibres will be noted. I am not able to quote from scientific laboratory comparisons of relative heat retaining qualities but by my judgement based on my own experiences. Natural fabrics are less prone to retain damp or odour from one's own body moisture which is constantly exuded, even in low temperature.

Thus lightly garbed we didn't just confine our journey to the Nurburgring in the Hartz mountains but carried on down through Austria across Northern Switzerland, before turning for home again through France. Only once did I feel the cold, and when I did it penetrated deep, from a howling crosswind we encountered when we were traversing the crest of some bald hills on a German Autobahn. To state that we were relying on clothing alone would be cheating as here I must confess we were both equipped with two of these remarkable little pocket warmers which operate in some mysterious way from lighter fuel without glow or danger of setting your clothing alight. These were stowed well down on our abdomens from which warmth spreads throughout the body. A cummerbund of some warm material might reasonably prove a substitute for an actual heating unit.

I have not yet dealt with those crucial extremities, feet and hands. From preference which has become a habit I wear leather riding boots winter and summer and for this arctic occasion they were treated with dubbin, a waterproofing substance that will endure efficiently when used with a full fairing which, of course, deflects water or slush thrown up by the front tyre. I doubt if there is any waterproofing agent which will stand up for more than an hour or two when subjected to high pressure treatment without a fairing or legshield when, desirably, you should employ overboot waders as rubber or plastic offers very little insulation on its own. Following a tip I picked up from goodness know's where, I wore a pair of my wife's discarded sheer stockings inside my woollen socks, fine weave for the occasion and not the hand knitted variety which would have become compressed inside my boots with dire effects on the circulation. I don't know the science behind the ladies' stockings — or could it have been sentimental? — but I did not suffer from cold feet on this most testing of journeys. Since I have never been greatly prone in this respect I can offer no guarantees that madam's nylons will work with everyone although my companion, Barry, was equally impressed with the results.

Hands are another matter, however. Mine freeze up within half an hour or so with fur lined gloves, deflective fairing and all. I have found the answer in electric gloves. These work most efficiently inside the extra insulation of waterproof over-mitts. They work on a very low wattage and the warmth provided is not discernable but, simply, they don't become cold. Before my acquaintance with electric gloves the most effective measure found to be a pair of rabbit skin mitts with the fur on the outside, and inside these I wore shetland wool mitts over thin silk gloves which were Royal Airforce Bomber Command surplus stock from World War 2. The RAF also used electric gloves made by the same people who supplied mine.

A new development is metal foil incorporated in the lining which was first tried and successfully tested inside space suits and which, according to the claim, provides quite exceptional insulation. Maybe these gloves are the answer but I have not yet spoken to anyone who has used them.

A useful tip when travelling on motorways in any country; at nearly all the gent's toilets (and presumably the ladies') which are provided in the service areas they use hot air blowers for drying the hands. So use these to warm the hands and the gloves as well. It is better to stop at every service area for a re-heat **before** the hands become numb as, if they do, it will not only be a painful process but it will require quite a long time before the circulation is fully restored — restored to the extent they will not freeze up again within a few minutes.

Saner types are less likely to want to tackle such extreme cold but on routes that include mountains or in Britain at anytime (remember the snowstorm that stopped the TT in June) one should be half way prepared to meet the unexpected.

There is one thing about which most highly experienced motorcyclists will agree and that is the most effective, nay, fully effective, type of rainwear. This is the two piece suit of heavy thornproof fabric which has been water proofed with a waxy substance which was first developed by Barbours for motorcycling and derived from their prior knowledge and experience in producing wet weather gear for the British navy. The pattern is now produced by many other manufacturers and the proven styling and material remains unchanged, despite the passage of many decades. *New Motorcylcing Monthly* (the magazine) carried out comparative controlled tests in a rain tunnel of all the popular styles of various materials and only the waxed thornproof withstood the high pressure deluge, equal to 17 inches of rain per hour, without letting in water. Two other suits of differing materials proved substantially waterproof but suffered from internal condensation and this was over a relatively short period of time.

No one in their right mind would attempt to ride through a deluge of this magnitude — I rather doubt if it

Attractive water-proof clothing such as this two-piece Belstaff suit is today's answer to the go-anywhere motorcyclist

Good quality leather boots are as important as a good crash helmet

For off-road riding this thornproof Belstaff suit is the answer

could be done in real life, for one thing the road would soon be awash. On the other hand this extreme, and to some extent, artificial test merely supports what I have found out from extensive practical experience in the real thing. Proofed nylon is fully water excluding but there is seepage through the stitched seams and it also suffers from condensation. Suits made of sheet plastic substances, sometimes simulated as leather, have welded seams and therefore should be fully waterproof but after a number of hours they become dripping wet internally, even when lined, and the moisture is transmitted back to one's clothing. Here I must mention that I am slim and do not perspire profusely. Yet, at the end of a long day encased in the thornproof variety, subjected to every type of wet globule found in nature, the inside lining has still felt dry to the touch. So why this apparent freedom from condensation? Presumably the material remains sufficiently porous to let fine vapour escape without, at the same time, letting coarser droplets in. I am only guessing. Of more importance to me is the reality that it keeps me dry on a motorcycle, the most wet inducing conveyance ever likely to be devised by man!

Unfortunately this is a tedious world in which there is always some vile snag to prevent a thing from being perfect. It is not the sort of garment which, in appearance or texture, makes one's chosen partner irresistibly embraceable. The very substance that causes water to flow off it like a duck's back feels greasy when warm and slightly tacky when cold and it attracts dust and grime as efficiently as it repels the rain drops. Shirts and blouses suffer from grubby cuffs and collars and it takes energetic laundering to remove the stain. Worst of all for the lady's pride and charm is the way the stuff gets under the fingernails as there seems no way of preventing the nails from going into mourning.

FEET AND HANDS

There are aerosol cans available of silicone compound that will waterproof leather and most other materials for a limited period of time but, leather boots so treated will not endure the bombardment of grit and water thrown up by the front wheel for very long. Personally I do not like rubber boots on their own and I much prefer waders that are pulled on over the leather riding boots, for prolonged riding in the rain. This combination is, however, somewhat bulky, restricting sensitivity in controlling the gear change lever and selection of the neutral position can become awkward. If you happen to be caught out lacking protective covering, a polythene bag will suffice but the thin variety will not last for long as the substance ages quickly and disintegrates from continuous flapping in the wind.

I would not put my trust in silicone as the exclusive remedy for keeping gloves waterproof for more than a very short period of time. Once wet through, the leather never quite regains its original suppleness and the overall life of the gloves is shortened. Fully waterproof overmitts are the answer, my choice being for the thornproof variety. A full width frontal fairing is a help but I have not found them to be fully effective during a prolonged run.

Water can run down the sleeves of the jacket into the cuffs of the overmitts. I have overcome this problem, by making bracelets of strips of rubber or plastic foam, the ends being stuck together with an impact adhesive. Two or three pulled over each sleeve, spaced about an inch apart above the cuff of the glove, work to perfection. They need to be of such circumference that they have to be stretched very slightly over the sleeve. They will last throughout the day once they are on, but the material does not stand up to repeated use, so make up spares while you are at it.

Once more, polythene bags will suffice as overmitts. The open end of the bag should be retained by a rubber band. If not available, try string, although this will tend to work its way off as it must be left fairly slack so that it does not feel tight on the arm or wrist. If you carry a passenger they can push all the open end slack up inside the sleeves, which is a lot easier than it sounds, and the process must be repeated following every occasion the rider needs the use of his unencumbered hands.

Obviously, riders eyes must be protected against rain and this applies even when a screen is fitted. A touring screen will deflect flying insects and snow up and over the head, but the updraught is insufficient to cope with rain drops. One can crouch behind the screen and look through it but visibility is not too good and one has to assume an uncomfortable riding posture. Consequently visors or goggles are the order of the wet day and these are subject to misting-up on the inside. My own choice for all occasions are goggles of flat shatterproof glass, which is free of distortion, with suede covered padding around the edge. Although these fit snugly to the face, one's moisture-bearing breath still finds its way inside as soon as one comes to a stop. There are anti-mist substances available which are effective although I have always mislaid the container at the time it is wanted, but almost any waxy or greasy substance will function if very thinly applied to the inside first by the finger and

Keeping warm at the Elephant Rally. This is claimed to be the coldest annual motorcycle event in Europe

Keeping cool in America

the surplus rubbed off with a cloth so that only a thin film remains. The process may need repeating in the course of a day.

An unbroken, leaden sky will of its own create a dreary landscape which does not inspire good cheer and it is this rather than the rain itself which lowers one's spirits and it becomes doubly depressing if one is wet into the bargain. On the other hand, if the cloud base is fairly high and there are bright glimpses I find that the miles roll by quite cheerfully and it is no great drag, particularly if I am dry and warm beneath the protective clothing. The virtue of pressing on regardless is that there is every prospect of breaking through into better weather. It is too bad if the depression is travelling along with you, as can happen, but one always takes refuge in hope.

A RIDING NOTE

Once a road surface has been sluiced off with enough water it ceases to be slippery and with the tyres we have today, the roadholding and braking is not greatly impaired. This is a generalisation which will apply to most road surfaces but you will need to be more keenly alert for greasy sections which the trained eye can distinguish from the mere glossy. In autumn, look out for leaves which might form a carpet — where there are adjacent farms be alert to cow pats. Both are mighty slippery when wet.

7 Motorcycle equipment for touring

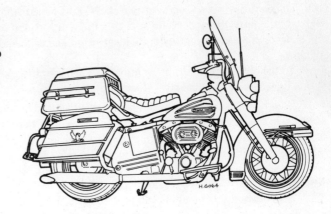

LUGGAGE ACCESSORIES

The seating arrangement and the springing of most motorcycles is calculated to result in the right weight distribution and handling characteristics for the rider plus one passenger. Yet very few makers or their designers seem really alert to the fact that the people who use them might actually want to carry changes of clothing and other impedimenta. This may be slightly overstating the case but inherently the motorcycle is not suited to carrying luggage equipment in any volume.

My own incursion into the field of luggage equipment followed my being a motorcyclist in the first place and being dissatisfied with the accessories available at the time. The traditional means was canvas bags which were strapped to a framework over the then unsprung rear wheel. The result was that the contents were churned and chafed and the frames prone to breakage over rough roads. A lot of riders preferred to carry their goods in knapsacks worn on their backs to the detriment of comfort and safety.

My original design consisted of quickly detachable cases, the dimensions of which were determined by what I considered to be right for the motorcycle, rather than the needs of rider and passenger, and carrying capacity was restricted accordingly. They were well reviewed in the journals and were a commercial success, but almost at once came the demand for something bigger. This I resisted on the basis that I knew what was good for them, or rather their motorcycles. Obviously, it was not long before there were imitators who did in literal fact enlarge on my ideas. This brought home the reality that it was preferable to compromise and give people what they wanted rather than be a bankrupt idealist!

I appear to remain among an apparent minority of motorcyclists who believe that one should trim one's luggage to suit the motorcycle, and no doubt my advice will go largely unheeded. Before considering what type of luggage carrying equipment will suit your needs, first consider what effect it will have on the safe or pleasurable handling of your machine and give some real thought to the minimum amount of luggage which you consider to be indispensable.

The influence of wind pressure must not be overlooked and whatever you add to a motorcycle, particularly at the rear end, will have some influence on its performance or handling. The bulkier the addition is, the greater will be the effect. But air is unpredictable stuff, ask any aerodynamicist, and even the same equipment on identical machines may behave differently, according to variations in the angles at which it is mounted, the weight or stance of the rider, or whether or not a fairing is fitted. But whatever the extent of the influence it is most unlikely to be of advantage. So far I have been talking only of the form and bulk of the equipment. Now add the weight when loaded and the affect on steering can become most noticeable; if heavily laden with a single rider, the bike will be prone to wobble alarmingly at low speed and weave at higher speeds, though a passenger, one who is an experienced riding partner, will substantially negate the adverse effect of heavy rear loading.

All this is certainly not intended to discourage the reader from fitting a luggage accessory of any sort; this would deprive them of being able to make full use of their machine. Luggage accessories are indispensable to the traveller and the snags and drawbacks need not be significant if they are wisely chosen in relation to the size of the model as well as the size of the rider and whether a passenger is normally carried.

Collectively or individually, people do try to carry way in excess of actual need. There are the obvious indispensables, the first being the toilet and sanitary gear to keep the body clean and beautiful. The contents will vary according to sex, age and foibles. All that I need add is that it is not necessary to carry the largest cake of soap, the fattest tube of toothpaste or a full wrap-around bath towel. The size and quantity of everything one takes needs consideration. Obviously keen swimmers will need to take bathing suits and most folk will want pyjamas.

In the choice of wardrobe an important consideration is that virtually all items are washable and drip dry. Avoid unnecessary duplication — if in doubt, leave it out.

Nearly all camp sites have self-laundering facilities but hotels and rooming houses expressly forbid clothes washing in the rooms. What they don't know they won't complain about, however, and a few items done discreetly without being allowed to drip on the carpets will harm no one. Take along a thin nylon clothes line and a few small plastic pegs if you can, as such a kit takes up little room and is not a superfluous luxury.

CARRIERS

Short distance commuters still have to carry things. Even fine weekenders are advised to carry rain gear in most places of this unpredictable world. A carrier on its own will meet these minimal requirements.

WINDSCREENS AND FAIRINGS

Very early in my motorcycling career I learned that man is not a streamlined creature who is designed by nature to hurtle through the air — and certainly not when sitting upright to face a gale or storm force wind. Since this early discovery, motorcycles have increased in speed, so we must now think in terms of hurricane force. This can be quite fun for a short blast off down a highspeed road (and if you are not worried about being caught by the law) while lying prone across the tank but the position itself is tiring and not suitable for long distance travel.

To me, the difference in having frontal air deflection is being able to cover 400 miles in a day and not feeling unduly fatigued, or feeling tired and being mighty stiff across the shoulders after 250 miles, when taking the full force of the air. This I confirmed to myself on the only long journey I have made in recent years on a naked machine, for this is how I regard them. This was on the Commando which I borrowed from Norton's for a test run to Spain. It was an impressive motorcycle and I must confess I could not resist zipping up to the ton in moments of exuberance, when the road conditions were inviting. Yet my sustained cruising speed declined very early in the day to below 60 mph, over highways which allowed for higher speeds with safety. This was during the first two days, when there was an imposed tight schedule, as I had an appointment to keep in Barcelona in the morning. I arrived in the late afternoon.

What type of fairing?

Even the simplest variety of windscreen consisting of a transparent blade fitted to supports which attach to the handlebars is highly effective, and deflects all frontal pressure to the extent that the slipstream will suck out the air behind, causing a depression, (a drop to below normal atmospheric air pressure) which in turn creates a slight updraught. The result is that if you are wearing a loose necktie it will be drawn out horizontal directly in front of you. This type of screen offers very little protection for the hands and does not prevent rainwater reaching the crutch.

The more modern (and expensive) type now in vogue consists of a transparent blade mounted above a wide fibre glass/plastic fairing, which gives substantial protection to the hands and upper part of the body.

The full fairing, to which the headlamp is transferred, is mounted by struts direct to the frame and it does not turn with the handlebars. This affords effective protection for the entire body including legs and feet, but waterproof clothing is still required when it rains. Although it deflects nearly all the water when the machine is in motion, the rain is as wetting as always when you come to a stop!

There are those who maintain that motorcycles fitted with windscreens and fairings become dangerous to handle in strong sidewinds. The fact is that any motorcycle becomes a handful in strong gusting winds, and winds do come in gusts along the average road as you ride out from a sheltered stretch into an exposed area. I cannot recall having had an particulary frightening experiences due to strong winds — I merely slow down enough to be able to control the thing and counteract the gusts in time by increasing the lean. One cannot avoid weaving to some extent, but have a look at what other road users are doing, particularly high sided trucks!

My conclusion is that there is nothing detrimental in fitting frontal protection other than one small snag to which the rider must become accustomed, namely that the screen deflects back a lot of engine noise. Consequently the rider is suddenly alerted to some fearsome clatterings and grindings which he had never noted before. One hardens to this and it is a small price to pay for comfort and freedom from muscular strain.

Make sure the contents to go into a pannier are first put into a polythene bag or they will scuff badly during transit

Craven Comet panniers and top case blend in nicely with this Honda CB550F Four

Aero elastics prove invaluable for securing top loads to the carrier

This machine is carrying too much in the wrong place for safe handling

Journalist Dave Minton makes use of his Swagman bags on this Honda Gold Wing

On this Gold Wing we have Krauser panniers, a large tank bag, a pair of Swagman bags and a rear carrier—a sensible way to distribute the load on this large machine. Note the use of balaclava helmets by the two riders in the background—silk is better than cotton

A different type of tank bag, sometimes known as an elephant bag, mounted on a Triumph X75 Hurricane

Not all panniers are of rigid construction. This design is quite flexible and looks neat

At one time, at least one manufacturer fitted a tank top carrier as standard. Today, this very useful fitment is almost unknown

Other than giving extra publicity to the manufacturer, it is difficult to determine what useful purpose a headlamp cover serves

This luggage has been stowed away more sensibly, using the portion of the dualseat usually occupied by the passenger to prevent overhang on the rear

It is possible to carry luggage safely without pannier cases, provided it is packed sensibly

Another type of screen, this time of French manufacture

A good example in the lower price category of a fairing made by Churchgate of Weymouth. A fairing such as this, not only deflects rain, but the wetting, high pressure jet, thrown back from the front wheel

Rickman panniers, rigid and compact, are the right size from the point of the bike and should not have a noticeable influence on handling. Fine for one rider but insufficient for two on a long tour. One snag - they are not quickly detachable - contents come out first!

The Craven-Mitchenall handlebar fairing is typical of many touring screens. This one incorporates a lockable compartment for a small quantity of luggage

Rickman panniers disguised as Honda. It is now very easy to buy 'matched' accessories for the more popular machines. Here is a Honda 750F1

A top case complements this Tower carrier and pannier set and helps to increase on carrying capacity

Tower pannier cases although capacious, are not quickly detachable without first removing the contents

Motorcycle Sport Editor Cyril Ayton, tries the latest R100RS BMW, which has a wind tunnel tested fairing as part of its overall specification

A Tower carrier on a Honda CB250

8 Coping with the physical hazards

H.606

THE FIRST AID KIT

I would put down a small first aid kit as a **must** when setting out on a tour and here I am not thinking of calamities, but the trivial little injuries which are quite likely to occur. For one thing, folk become more accident prone in small ways when on tour, contending with matters outside their normal beat — or certainly this is how it applies to me. At the last moment one puts on a spurt to prepare the bike for the road and when carrying out an adjustment to a mirror or attaching the luggage one commits some stupidity, like gouging a piece out with one's own thumbnail or catching a finger against a knobbly piece of the bike that has always been there. Or there's opening a sardine tin with an old fashioned tin opener (the little lever thing having been lost or omitted), oh! the right combinations for self inflicted wounds are limitless.

Burns are a hazard to which motorcyclists are particularly susceptible and I have in mind hot exhaust pipes. A sear against the lady's exposed calf is particularly common and it leaves a nasty raw area that is slow to heal. It needs to be covered to prevent infection. A good first aid kit will include a suitable medicament and dressing for burns.

SUNBURN

If you are travelling south to the Mediterranean area or any place where the sun is intense, and that could include England too, take this seriously unless you are among the lucky who tan easily. In these circumstances I dare not ride in a short sleeved shirt and I wear gloves, as a scorched back of the twistgrip hand can be very painful. Take suitable lotions for prevention and treatment. Consult your chemist and don't fall for buying the most expensive thing. Nothing will stop my nose from becoming raw and peeling but it would probably be a lot worse if I did not try to allay the havoc. Lip salve is another of my needs or they crack and bleed after several days of riding, regardless of the weather.

SUNGLASSES

Along with the majority of others I need the relief of sunglasses in brilliant southern sun. But remember they are habit forming; that the eye quickly develops a tolerance which makes their need greater with less relief to be gained. Accordingly, do not wear them as a matter of habit and remember to take them off when the sun is well past its zenith. For obvious reasons, the type with unbreakable lenses should be used for motorcycling and my choice is the Polaroid variety, for which the claim is made that they exclude the dangerous rays and dazzle without resorting to very dark tints. Select a cheerful tint, dark yellow in particular makes all clouds look thunderous and threatening.

COLIC

This is a grim and painful malady that faces all those who travel south in summer. The little bug that causes it flourishes in hot climates and develops a strength that forces our pale northern phagocytes to go into rapid retreat and it takes them a day or two to gather strength and reform the ranks. The results can be extreme; acute diarrhoea, with frequent vomiting and intestinal cramp which comes in spasms, mounting to a dreadful intensity. In Mexico it is referred to as the Aztec Two Step or Montezuma's Revenge. The victim hopes he will

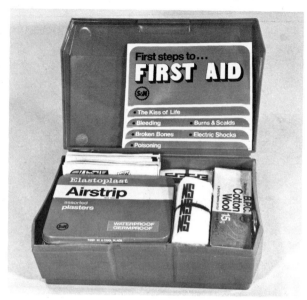

Always carry a first aid kit. This is a complete, moderately priced kit that is easy to carry

Two sizes of special aerosol treatment for insect bites and wasp and bee stings are featured

Sunglasses are better than tinted visors or goggles; they provide less distortion for a given glare resistance

Different lotions, creams and oils suit different skins. Try to take one which you know works for you

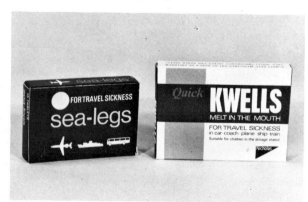

Travel sickness often causes extreme hardship to those who suffer

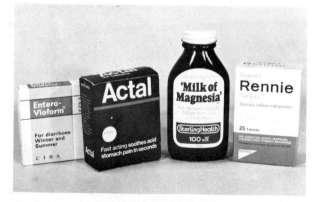

Actual travelling as well as strange food can cause discomfort to many people. Find the treatment which will help you

die, but in the back of his mind is the fear that he won't! Take heart; after rising to a crescendo it will gradually diminish, though leaving you rather weak and feeling feverish for a day or two afterwards.

There are tablets available which will expedite the recovery and can also be used as a preventative, if taken regularly during one's journey. I recently read a medical denunciation of a continued preventive course because of possible harmful side effects. (What medicine hasn't?). Seek the advice of your chemist, if you have faith in his advice.

An article I read, by a Doctor, stated it was easy to avoid colic by refraining from eating certain foods (all of them delectable) and always carrying a bottle of dilute permanganate with which to clean drinking glasses and cutlery with a damp cloth. Imagine the face of the waiter when you try that on at a posh restaurant!

The washing of fresh fruit does make sense and most continental restaurants issue bowls of water for this purpose. Avoid over-ripe fruit, particularly peaches and figs, as these become a breeding ground for bugs once the skin has been damaged.

Beware of foods on which flies have settled, as they are carriers. A few precautions make sense but follow all the rules and you will not fade away from undernourishment!

Know your allergies. A bee or wasp can cause a wide area of pain and swelling with a tendency to black out. Make sure of having anti-hystamine tablets available — they can only be had on prescription as they have side-effects and make one sleepy.

It is a lucky person who does not have a particular weakness or susceptibility and it is not pandering to one's hypochondria to take along the prescribed antidote. For heaven's sake declare your allergies to your companions so that others will know. From a past experience I know I should not be given an anti-tetanus injection. Accordingly I had a disc engraved which I wore on a wristlet but which, of course, I have managed to loose.

A diabetic has to be particularly careful. On one occasion we were just about to set off when a fellow joined our small group from the other hotel. We asked him where his riding partner was. "Must have gone on ahead with another group as he hasn't shown up". He answered. Something was wrong. You get a feeling for it. So over we went to find that his key had not been handed in to Reception. We eventually found him flat out, unconscious on his bed. A doctor was sent for, who charged us 20 Swiss Francs for disagreeing that he was in a diabetic coma. We searched his luggage in the admission room at the hospital and there it was; a syringe and insulin ampoules. He caught us up and passed by mid-afternoon, and seemed most aggrieved in the evening, when we tore a strip off him.

So there we have it. Prepare for lacerations, splinters, spikes, stings and excruciating gripes, but remember that there are pharmacies in all countries. Throughout most of Europe they carry extensive stocks and the pharmacists themselves can be very helpful and knowledgeable with advice about the treatment or medicaments required.

Tyre changing is not always accomplished under the best of conditions or at the most convenient time

9 Ken – and the art of motorcycle maintenance

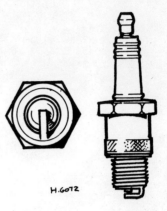

H.GOTZ

In my younger days when the two motorcycle weeklies were proper magazines I was an avid reader of the regular workshop columns. Over a time the effect of these was calculated to have similar consequences to reading Everyman's Medical Encyclopaedia when the sanest man becomes a shattered hypochondriac. These workshop articles assumed that experienced motorcyclists were ever alert to sounds and symptoms of a host of troubles. My ear became attuned to every fresh frequency which denoted bent valve stems, seized piston rings, a broken roller, an oilway blockage. I would then take a long screwdriver, the most handy instrument for use as a stethoscope, and holding the handle against my ear I would probe various parts of the engine with the working end. This would prove the worst, that the engine was on the point of disintegration!

But on my 55 mile daily journey winter and summer to and from my place of work I slowly became less obsessional and stopped listening for funny noises which are inherent in every engine. In fact, I developed a fresh outlook, that if the whole device is running sweetly and without loss of power it is far better to leave it alone — but within reason.

Every powered road going contrivance suffers from continuous wear and tear and requires routine maintenance to ensure reliability and to prolong its overall life. Even though it may be running well there comes a time after a lot of mileage when a full inspection and overhaul becomes a wise precaution, including the renewal of apparently sound components. The effect of expansion and contraction from heat, thrusting, grinding and whirling results in wear, loss of tension or internal but invisible fatigue, and there is a life expectancy for certain parts beyond which it is pushing your luck.

Now that I have reached a balanced sense of proportion (thousands will probably disagree) I propose to outline what I regard as feasible and important, based on my own experiences, and with particular reference to preparation for a long trip away from home base. I have no intention of overwhelming the novice so I hope I will not arouse too many scoffs from the expert. Maybe I can surprise them too about some aspects that they have not considered.

TYRES

"Tyres wear more rapidly on a tour than in daily use" — true, or false? I cannot avoid again saying the answer depends on circumstances, which vary, but the causes of wear do not. These are the stresses caused by acceleration, braking and cornering: and the rate at which these stresses take their toll is increased enormously with the rise in the temperature of the tyre rubber. Sustained high speed will also result in rapid wear, as will be explained later. The individual who has planned his tour, can now compare the conditions he anticipates meeting, with those of his daily life. If his usual mileage is 100 miles a week, and his tour is 2,000 miles long, he is for that reason alone concentrating 20 weeks of speed, acceleration and braking wear into the one short period. Exaggerating to make the point clear, his home mileage might consist of a straight, flat road where he accelerates for a few seconds at the beginning, brakes at the end, and puts no further strain on the tyre whatsoever. The tour will include — he fervently hopes — warm weather, longer than usual periods of continuous riding, some fast stretches, and above all the extra weight of luggage and perhaps a companion, all of which will add to the tyre temperature and so increase the effect of the stresses. If these too are increased because of the nature of the roads to be covered, the difference between tyre wear on the tour, and what he has been used to at home, can be

Check hydraulic brake fluid level in handlebar mounted reservoir

XS500C model has separate rear brake reservoir, above brake pedal

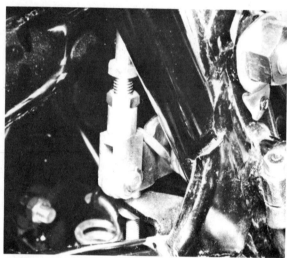

Adjuster for rear brake pedal travel (XS500C model)

Aerosol-type lubricants permit chain to be lubricated in-situ

Electrolyte must be between these two levels (battery shown is unfilled)

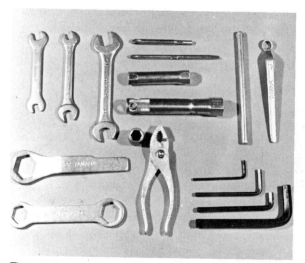

The complete tool kit supplied with the XS500C model

These two pages of photographs are taken from the Haynes Owners Workshop Manual for the Yamaha 500 dohc Twins as being a typical example of the type of maintenance needed for a twin cylinder motorcycle

Brake pad wear can be checked by raising flap

Also applies to rear brake of XS500C model

Check tyre pressures with a gauge known to be accurate

Check contact breaker gaps with feeler gauge

Use a dipstick to check oil level

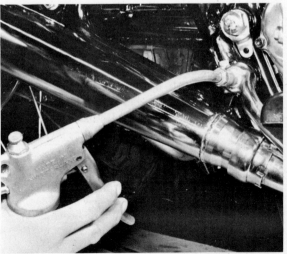

Do not omit to grease swinging arm pivot

dramatic. I learned this when I was loaned a works Commando, which recorded only 1,500 miles when I took it over. After 2,000 miles of a test run down to Spain the tread was almost down to the bone!

A motorcycle tyre is produced with very deep treads, which allow for a lot of wear and when as much as two-thirds is worn off, it will probably retain plenty of grip and the extent of wear will not be apparent unless compared to a new one. If in doubt, it is not difficult to make the comparison, perhaps by just walking around the machines displayed in or in front of a local motorcycle dealer's shop, with one's own parked nearby.

It is no loss to replace a part-worn tyre if this is done in advance: it can be put aside for use at a later date. In fact, if monetary inflation continues, it can be a tax free capital gain! Punctures, though happily rare these days, still occur; and they become the more likely the thinner the amount of rubber left — well before the moment when grip starts to be lost and the legal limit of acceptable wear approaches.

The commonest cause of a puncture is a nail dropped perhaps by a farm vehicle. Modern roads have fewer nails than existed in earlier days and more vehicles to mop them up. But perhaps the planned tour includes stretches with few vehicles, and a lot of nails! The touring motorcycle of today is unlikely to have the virtues of older British models, where a wheel could be removed, the tube changed and inflated, and the rider on his way again within 15 minutes. There is another inflexible rule about punctures, which all who have suffered one will confirm: they always occur in a remote spot, in the middle of a thunderstorm, just after one's riding companion has disappeared around the corner ahead! How much simpler to reduce the chances by checking both tyres in advance, and renewing them if necessary. The rear tyre is the more susceptible to wear; the front one the more vital to safety. So both need to be looked at.

The theory of the pneumatic tyre is that it requires a definite quantity of air, at normal temperature and pressure, to support a given load. By use of a pump, a large amount of air is forced into the small volume of the tyre, thus raising its pressure. That is what tyre pressure is all about. The recommended pressure as listed in the Makers handbook, represents the amount of air necessary to support the weight of the machine, an average rider, a tank full of petrol — but probably not that of a passenger plus the luggage.

By support, the Manufacturer means a pressure which will keep the tyre cool and in good shape, yet offer enough resilience to give a comfortable ride. In the old days of rigid framed machines, the tyre was a major source of comfort (the seat providing the only other one) so that to achieve a sufficient volume of air and yet leave acceptable resilience, tyres tended to be of larger section, to permit lower pressures. With the development and improvement of sprung suspension systems, tyres could be made narrower and pumped up harder; but this does not alter the fact that they need to be pumped harder still if the air is going to give proper support to a heavier-than-usual load.

As the motorcycle (or indeed any other vehicle using tyres) proceeds, the wheel turns. The small area of tyre in contact with the road carries the entire weight of machine and its load, and is compressed. An instant later, this section moves away from the road, the pressure is released and the tyre springs out: in a word, it flexes. This constant flexing is the main source of heat build up in the tyre. If an extra load is not compensated for by higher pressure, the tyre will flex more deeply and greater heat will be generated. The faster the machine travels, the more rapid will be the flexing. It is easy to see, therefore, that if a machine is both ridden at speed, and its tyres are under-inflated, the build-up of heat can become prodigious, and wear extremely rapid. This build-up is not arithmetic: 60 mph does not result in twice the build-up of 30 mph, but a great deal more than that. This is something that is easily tested: put a hand on the tyre after a run. But try it carefully, it could be hot enough to burn your fingers! This, incidentally, explains why all handbooks say that pressures should be checked before setting out when the tyre is cold. The tyre manufacturers issue lists of commended types and tyre pressures for individual makes and models but fail to mention the variables in pressures depending on their loading and use. One manufacturer does stipulate that pressure should be increased in the rear tyre by 3 lb psi when a pillionist is carried. I will go further than this and suggest that yet an additional 1 lb should be added to the rear tyre for each 10 lbs of luggage carried, not forgetting the weight of the panniers themselves. This is only a rough guide and the final guideline should be what feels right as well as looks right — if a tyre flattens out noticeably on its weight bearing area of the road surface, it is fairly certain to be under-inflated. Another thing, manufacturers stipulate higher pressures for the very fast motorcycles but not all fast motorcycles are consistently driven fast. If the bulk of one's driving is to and from work through built up areas, it is reasonable enough to drop the pressures by a few pounds, for greater comfort and increased adhesion particularly during winter months when roads can be greasy. It is rather a matter of commonsense and personal experience and you will be safe enough if you do not deviate too widely from the manufacturer's advice. Nor, if you do as I do, will you take a pressure reading every day even on a long tour, it is enough to check between finger and thumb to know that pressure is being maintained.

Furthermore, when you push on a tyre gauge you will almost certainly let out a little air, perhaps as much as 2 lb and every time you replace air there is the prospect of conveying in a particle of grit which can lodge under the seat of the valve and make the whole air content come rushing out. Get the air pressure right before you start out on a journey and leave it alone as long as you are comfortable and the vehicle is handling consistently. Another aspect about tyres, there are now several types and tread shapes — take care when you replace just one tyre that it should match the other. A bargain tyre which is a mismatch is no bargain at all if it results in disconcerting or dangerous handling.

ROUTINE MAINTENANCE

The relative trouble-free aspect of modern machines should encourage today's motorcyclist, who may perhaps have heard hoary tales from former days, and wonder how we dared venture more than a few miles from home ground. On the other hand, it is possible to be over-encouraged, to realise that the picture I have just drawn has little apparent relevance to his own experience, and therefore to be misled into carrying neglect altogether too far. A modern motorcycle, setting out in good condition, may be expected to complete the most arduous holiday tour without further attention than to the tyres and chains soon to be mentioned. But if it is not in good condition, if it has been ridden for a long while, and particularly if it is largely used for very short journeys, then potential failures must be considered. And with the modern motorcycle, their repair by the roadside may be quite impossible.

In a phrase, don't be frightened off by old men's tales: but neither be overconfident and forget that a machine is a machine....Therefore I recommend:

DAILY INSPECTION

Tyres I cannot stress this too strongly: they are your link with the road surface and therefore with your life. Don't glance — look! For low pressure, for possible bits of flint or nails in and between the treads, for missing valve caps which can let in grit and lead to abrupt deflation. Occasionally look for signs of tyre creep. To do this, slacken off the finger nut securing the valve stem to the wheel. If the valve then tips out of vertical, you have creep, which requires attention; a bit more of it and the valve could pull right off and be cut by the rim, resulting in an instant flat. This is very rare, but needs only to happen once in a lifetime, to shorten that life-time!

Chains For correct tension.

Oil level As well as just petrol.

Battery water level This is a 'must' at the end of the first long day out, since if there is an inherent tendency to overcharge, this may be the first time that it shows up. If all is well, occasional rather than daily checks should suffice for the rest of the tour. Top up with distilled water, when required.

Lights Check that all are working correctly, so that faults can be corrected **before** dark. Include trafficators and brake lights.

Screws, nuts and bolts It is usually enough to check nuts by hand in preference to a wrench. This is a generalisation rather than a rule but whenever tools are used to check for tightness, they should be employed with discretion to avoid moving a threaded component which is already tight enough.

Wheel spokes I always check for loose spokes out of old habit. I do it by hand. Some people like to run a stick or pencil around them; if they go ping-ping-ping-phut, the phut will denote a loose spoke. In which case take great care not to over-tighten. Wheel building is a skilled business and you could end up with a wobbly or oblong rim by excess or unnecessary tensioning of spokes. So, by turning the spoke nipple which protrudes through the rim, take up the tension just enough to restore a slight ping rather than a resonant one.

All cables Check for signs of fraying and ensure that they are lubricated.

Control levers Check among other things that they are doing their job and take up undue free play. Actually I like a fair amount of free movement of the front brake lever for more delicate control, but it must be able to come on fully.

General Walk slowly round the machine looking closely at every part. Establish a routine for this.

How long will all this take? — An adequate inspection should not take longer than five minutes. More time will be needed, of course, if faults are found but nothing like as long as if those faults are neglected. Those five minutes may well save you a tedious or even dangerous experience later in the day. Incidentally, I carry out an equally appropriate drill when I am travelling by car and I am rewarded, if that is the word, by occasionally discovering failings which need remedying on the spot, quite apart from routine matters like topping up the engine oil or the battery.

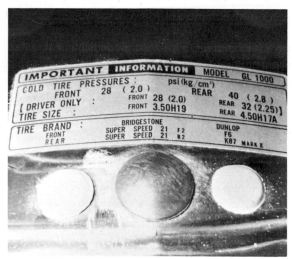

Always maintain tyre pressures correctly

Check electrolyte level in battery

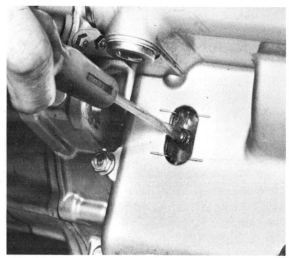

Clean sight glass to view oil level and ...

... top up engine, if necessary

Adjust clutch after removing inspection cover

Maintain coolant level in reservoir

These two pages of photographs are taken from the Haynes Owners Workshop Manual for the Honda GL 1000 Gold Wing as being reasonably typical of the type of maintenance needed for a four cylinder motorcycle or one with shaft drive

Check fluid level in BOTH master cylinder reservoirs

Air filter housed in box within dummy fuel tank

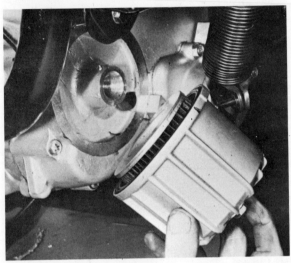

Fit new filter element replacing ...

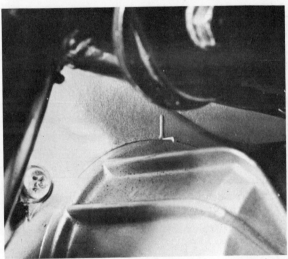

... the housing so that the marks line up

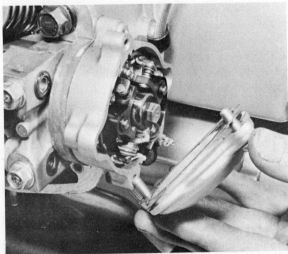

Remove contact breaker assembly cover to ...

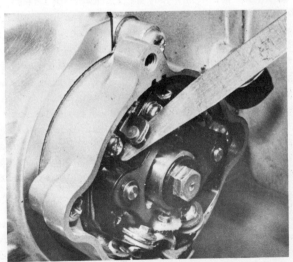

... allow inspection and adjustment of points

SUGGESTED SPARES

My concern here is to have the tools and the spares to be able to cope with possible failures, within my capacity to rectify at the roadside, which could bring me to a stop. It is galling, usually inconvenient, and often expensive, to be helplessly immobilised for lack of some small item.

Cables Failure of clutch or throttle cables will bring most riders and their machines to a complete stop. I have managed with a broken throttle cable by yanking at the remnant which I twisted round two fingers of my right hand and it is possible to progress without a clutch, if you bump start after a stop. You can even change gear when in motion if you time it carefully. But these are temporary measures and you would be very lucky indeed to be able to keep going until you found a source of spares. So take these with you or, better still, fit the new ones and take the old as spares. This way you will be certain that they fit and so avoid the prospect, humans being imperfect, that you have been issued with cables for the right model but the wrong year or that a big blob of solder makes it impossible to fit without filing it off and you don't have a file! Front brake cables seldom break but as this is your main stopper, it is worthwhile carrying a spare — without it you could be dangerously handicapped.

Tyre valve caps and cores, and a means of extracting a faulty core if this is not included with the cap. Chain spring link, even if the machine in question is fitted with a continuous type of chain. A broken link can still be wrenched off even without a proper extractor, and be replaced with one of these.

Tyre repair equipment A pump, a puncture repair outfit and two small tyre levers. These are adequate if you go about it the right way. The centre of the wheelrim is recessed, that is, it is of smaller diameter than the outer rim. This is known as the well. When a tyre is deflated, it is a simple matter to ease one section of the beading into the well when the section directly opposite can be levered off without excessive muscle. The alternative, or perhaps an addition, is to carry an aerosol-type inflating device which also includes a liquid giving a temporary seal to the puncture. Vinilec is the Trade name for one of these. I personally have never bothered as they merely postpone temporarily the need for a full repair and involves the replacement of the inner tube itself, although I can see its value on a dark and stormy night. I would also advocate that you study the means of extracting the rear wheel in advance and not leave it to despair over when the dismal occurence takes place.

Toolkit as issued with the bike, adding a good pair of pliers if these are not included.

Instruction manual

Wire a couple of feet of soft annealed wire for emergency lash-ups.

Insulating tape

Fuses (Silver paper wrapped round a blown one will conduct electricity and restore power to those machines where everything stops with the loss of a single fuse. The aid should be used with caution, however. A fuse is a safety device, which may have failed for reasons other than mere old age....)

Light bulbs Although I always carry a spare headlight bulb, in all the years I have been riding I have not blown one yet. I grant they are pretty vital on a dark night but if both filaments blow, one after the other, I doubt if a spare would endure long either as it would indicate that something is drastically wrong with the electrics. Here I can impart one piece of advice. If there is a sudden surge upwards in light intensity with increased engine revs. it could indicate a flat or failing battery but it could, more seriously (from the aspect of blowing the bulb) be the result of a corroded or faulty earth from the battery to the machine. Small bulbs, particularly speedometer lights in my experience, have a limited life. A failure of any of the auxiliaries should not bring you to a stop, though being without a tail light is illegal anywhere, so I carry these as spares to save shopping around and I reckon they will be used at some time in the future.

Special spares Despite all progress, there can be very few machines which do not have their own particular weak points. These can be discovered the hard way through long personal experience, but even this information can be usefully augmented through a chat with other owners of a like model, or the dealer who sold it will tell you — **after** you have bought the bike! Add your own special spares suggested by the information.

CHAINS

Motorcyclists, as a breed, don't like chains, and greatly prefer to pretend that they do not exist. Take any well used and generally well cared for machine, of any make, model or year: if there is a fault in its maintenance, the chances are high that it will lie with the chain. Alas, chains do exist: and can be particularly troublesome if they go wrong far from home, in a strange country, with a time schedule already showing signs of strain. It is sometimes overlooked, perhaps precisely because it is so obvious when one thinks about it, that a chain consists of a larger number of plain metal bearings. As we all know, bearings need oil — but chain bearings don't always get it. The movement of the chain round the sprockets tends to throw the oil off; but there is enough left to act as a glue, collecting from the dusty air and particularly from wet and muddy minor roads, a highly effective abrasive medium. This works its way into the rollers which are the chain's bearings, and wear follows with increasing rapidity. This results in a growing gap between the inner and outer rollers of the chain link, permitting more abrasive to get in. Invariably one section of chain wears more rapidly than the rest, which is further aggravated by a whip lash effect. Nevertheless a chain should never be allowed to run dry and if the machine is not equipped to provide automatic lubrication of the chain or if the volume is not adequate, then oiling should be undertaken as a regular chore after a previous day's long run. There are now aerosols with special chain oils available to make this task simple and less messy.

If the self-destroying aspect of chains sounds frightening, remember that this applies too to virtually all other moving parts, although the rate of wear is generally less rapid. If you don't look after them, you will have to resign yourself to renewing them at intervals, just as you do with tyres. I cannot possibly quote a figure in terms of mileage as so much depends on the power of the engine and the treatment it has to take; above all it will depend on the extent of maintenance it receives and it is still the Achilles heel in this respect. It does, in fact, demand a fair degree of attention to provide long and reliable service.

The first rule of all is to maintain correct adjustment. The makers will have listed the amount of up and down movement of the chain at the centre of its run as the test for correct tensioning. They will also have said — a vital point this — that the test should be made at the tightest point; implying that there will also be looser areas where wear has begun. The springing of the rear wheel as it moves up and down will itself result in a slight variation of chain tension, tightening and loosening constantly as the suspension does its job of absorbing road shocks. If the chain has been wrongly tensioned to give the correct amount of movement at its loosest instead of its tightest spot there is the prospect of it snapping, which can be catastrophic. At best it will deposit itself gently on the road, leaving the rider to wonder why his power has suddenly disappeared and, if it has drifted off the surface it might involve quite a search to retrieve it! A broken chain has been known to tangle round the rear sprocket, jam against the frame and then lock the wheel, with the result that machine and rider descend painfully to earth.

Of equal importance comes periodic cleaning, which calls for removal, immersion and agitation in paraffin (kerosene to you Americans). More dedicated motorcyclists will have two chains, the spare one being left in a container covered with heavy duty oil and hung up a full day before installation, to allow surplus oil to drain off. Alternatively, and more effective, is immersion in a special grease, one that can be melted without deteriorating, which is heated until it becomes liquid, then 'cooked' for about 10 minutes, during which time it should be stirred with a stick to aid penetration. The chain should be removed and suspended until it cools off, so that surplus liquid grease will drain off before refitting. This is a somewhat messy operation which is unpopular with wives (or Mothers) if it is done in the kitchen, employing a treasured cooking utensil. One period in my early married life was blighted by such an occasion. Yet given such attention a pair of chains could well endure until the motorcycle itself requires a complete overhaul. And when is a chain worn out and needing replacement? I will now quote a section of a useful Renold leaflet 'Chain care for the motorcyclist'.

"Wear up to a ¼ inch per foot of chain length is accommodated by the depth of hardening of the bearing surfaces and when this limit is reached the chain should be replaced. With a new 5/8 inch pitch chain, 16 pitches will come to the 10 inch mark on the rule, and a sufficiently accuracte check for subsequent wear is to take a limit of 10 7/32 inches for 16 pitches. In the case of a ½ inch pitch chain, 23 pitches will come to the 11½ inch mark on the rule and the limit of 11¾ inches for 23 pitches should be taken as the maximum permissible wear."

To carry out this check, they recommend that the chain is removed and cleaned but not oiled and then placed on a board. One end should be anchored by a nail and the chain pulled out to its full extent and measured in sections.

All this is useful technical knowledge if you want to be scientific about it. For my part the variation in chain wear will tell me what I want to know. If the chain is correctly tensioned at its tight spot and sags down to an unacceptable extent where it is slackest, then I feel the time has come to say farewell. This, however, is a matter for discretion and involves an element of experience. If you don't throw away a chain in good time it can cause sprockets to wear, when the teeth will assume a hooked appearance. The vehicle will then require new sprockets as well, or your new chain will become quickly worn, perhaps in just a few hundred miles. All this can be a costly business and it is one of the blunders I have managed to avoid.

If you have not been a maintenance minded fellow, my advice about the chain is the same as for tyres — if in doubt fit a new one before setting out on a long tour. If the old one has any life left in it you will then have

Top-up oil tank level if ...

... below level of sight glass

Check gearbox oil level and replenish

Press red button if engine is hot ...

... remove cap and check level

Fluid level must ALWAYS be correct

These two pages, and page 86, of photographs are taken from the Haynes Owners Workshop Manual for the Suzuki 750 3 Cylinder as being typical of the type of maintenance needed for a two-stroke motorcycle

... move spindle equally each side

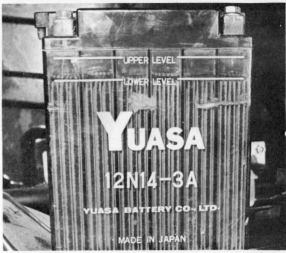

Check electrolyte is between level marks

Carburettor adjustment here is incorrect

Oil pump arm line must slign when ...

... throttle is in this position

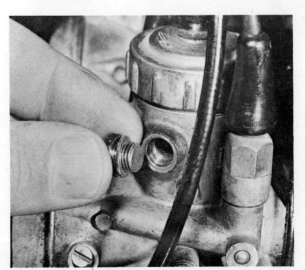

Plug gives access to aligning mark

Adjust rear brake at cable rod end

Use a proprietary chain lubricant

Use chain adjuster draw bolts to tension chain

two and this could well be the start of a new approach. Perhaps the new approach will be to rush off and buy a BMW or other shaft drive model! For my part I sometimes cuss chains but I still find them tolerable.

In my peak days when I was virtually wedded to my motorcycle — Mollie avers I would have taken the model to bed with me had it not been for the sharp bend at the top of the stairs. My machines were average examples of British machinery of the time which is to say they had bugs built into them from the design stage and augmented during manufacture. Let us be fair, however, they were basically sturdy vehicles of many virtues and the failings were minor irritants, rarely serious and hardly ever beyond the remedy of a person with modest mechanical sense. With most models it was a constant battle against oil seepage; tappets, ignition points, voltage regulators, carburettors, anything that could get out of adjustment did so at varying intervals. Then there were a few more drastic failings specific to certain models such as Triumphs built during a particular year which sometimes suffered broken wheel spokes (a serious matter this as a chain reaction takes place unless replacements are quickly installed), Sunbeams and a broken primary chain tensioner and Vincent slipping clutches. On others, important springs were liable to fracture, some chewed up certain control cables, most had their idiosyncracies. Virtually all could shed nuts and bolts unless they were regularly checked and tightened and the durability of electrical equipment was not all that could be desired.

This makes a gloomy picture but it becomes exaggerated in the telling for, with all, these failings did not amount to serious unreliability although they could be relied on to occur. In reality it was merely a matter of daily maintenance when on a tour and rectification at the time it was needed. This was accepted philosophically as part of life's routine, like grooming and dressing after getting up in the morning, and the great virtue of these machines was that they were simple and within the realms of human understanding without specialised training. Of about 1,400 motorcycles that accompanied us abroad over the years, I can recall only two which developed mechanical failings, outside of mishaps, which resulted in their having to be conveyed back by other means, and both these bikes had started out in a rather worn condition.

The modern motorcycle is generally a less temperamental piece of equipment, but it is still liable to wear and requires maintenance. The great difference between the modern bike and its predecessors, is not what happens in the course of its life, but how quickly, and how much daily attention is called for.

Screw top oil cans are fairly rare these days. They are the only answer for carrying oil on a motorcycle

10 Stretching your money in Europe

As I am writing this the Pound has been taking a beating and consequently it will buy more at home than it will abroad or, conversely you will find things — but still not all things — more expensive when you leave these shores. Presumably, however, equilibrium will be established in the end although almost certainly by British prices increasing to revert to the **status quo antes**. Fortunately, this is not likely to affect most motorcyclists, who are mainly of the younger age groups and whose incomes tend to keep pace roughly with the rate of inflation.

In dealing with how to make your money go further, which for the time being has a special relevance, I should make it clear that it has always cost more, or at best the same, to take a two or three weeks Continental tour than the equivalent in Britain. This was still so when the Pound was a desirable currency. The reason for this is the inevitable cost of the Channel crossing and Insurance, presuming you are wise enough to take out additional cover (see final chapter). Despite this, tens of thousands of British motorcyclists once toured Continental Europe every summer until, by the mid 60's, their numbers began to wane. This had nothing to do with the economy, which was booming, but the transition to the motor car and the temporary decline of the motorcycle.

Recently, there has been a resurgence of interest and it would be a sad thing if the desire to travel abroad had to be curtailed because of its cost. On the other hand, a little knowledge can go part of the way to help reduce the extra expense.

Petrol in most European countries has nearly always cost more than in Britain for as long as I can remember. Most cross channel services permit you to carry a full tank, so do so. Fill it right up to the very top and come back empty, but don't miss the boat by running dry in the last mile! If you are going through more than one country bear in mind that the price can vary widely from one country to another and take advantage of this accordingly.

Having met the initial expense of taking your bike over, it would seem foolish to restrict your mileage because of fuel costs. It is worth saving for, surely? But there are ways of getting better mileage in return for a little restraint. Vivid acceleration and high speeds gulps a disproportionate amount of fuel. It is hard to suggest this to the owner of a Superbike, with a demoniacal thirst at the best of times, as he has bought it for power and wants to use it. Yet it is not essential to drive competitively all the time, least of all on the open road. A gradual build-up of speed rather than zip acceleration can result in a very useful saving in the course of imposed variations in speed, several hundred times each day. Another waster is last moment braking, when coming to a halt. There is generally plenty of advance warning which calls for slowing down or stopping. Shut off early and all the distance you have coasted is a free bonus. And how fast is fast? I can give no figure here as motorcycles have widely varying performances, even within their own categories of engine size. Speaking from impression of most of the machines I have ridden, the first one-third of the throttle opening turns on about two-thirds of the engine's potential power and this can produce a very high rate of knots from the big fellows. For the rest of the movement in the twist grip you will have an increase in petrol consumption without a corresponding return in power or speed. All that I am trying to put across here is that it is not necessary to use more than one-third of the twist grip movement to tap a high percentage of performance available to you.

For an economical sustained cruising speed, one-third throttle is probably too much with most models, a quarter is more likely and perhaps less for the Superbike, which will really shift along at this setting and consume a lot of fuel in combating air pressure. In fact, the greatest mileage which can be achieved with almost any vehicle is right down at the bottom of the scale, with the engine ticking over just above the point where it will snatch. If you are out to break records, don't vary the throttle setting but use the gears to cope with variations in gradient. This is not particularly good for an engine designed to turn over briskly and can be even worse for your temper, but it is something to remember when you are down to reserve and you don't know how far you are from the next filling station.

How much fuel can you save without going to the extreme? Obviously there can be no arbitrary figure but I think the average rider will find that it requires only a modicum of restraint and sacrifice in speed to achieve a 10% saving. Let me put it the other way round, which is a useful ploy to prove a point. We'll assume a fairly brisk rider who does not hang around but still allows a safety margin to spare and does not overstretch his machine (in all modesty I have myself in mind). He normally gets a return of, say, 50 mpg on his journey to work, but then comes the day when he leaves slightly later and has to make up a few minutes. Without overdoing it, his mileage drops to 45. On the occasions when he has to push it right to the limit, gulp! it will drop right down to 40 or even less. I doubt if many people will quarrel with this example unless it is regarded as an underestimation.

The cost of petrol has risen faster than almost any other commodity and will be the major outlay for a longish tour with an averagely thirsty model. This is where a saving can really amount to something and it is usually so easy to achieve.

Lubricating oil in some countries can be very expensive. It is usually sold in 2 litre cans and, as one never needs this quantity for topping up, one is left with a somewhat bulky container in which to transport the surplus. Best thing is to start the journey with a quart of oil in a screw top container which, in itself, will prove adequate for topping up a four stroke motorcycle in good condition for an entire tour of 2,000 miles or so.

As with petrol, certain things have always cost more over the channel — other things still cost less despite the slide in the Pound (as there are many countries in Europe there are bound to be exceptions so I'll quote France, the largest country and our closest neighbour). Costing more are meat, most tinned and packaged foods, butter, restaurant meals, tea, coffee whether the ingredients or served as refreshment, imported fruits (i.e. bananas) soft drinks. Worst buy: continental breakfast.

Generally costing less are regional fruits and vegetables, particularly if obtained in markets, tobacco, alcoholic drinks (except imported spirits) and overnight accommodation, meaning just the rooms without meals.

The cost of tea or coffee at cafes is disproportionately expensive so one needs to cut down on refreshment stops. To me this is a sacrifice, as one of my pleasures is to sit at a table on the pavement, absorb the atmosphere and watch the world go by.

It is still worth it when you have the time to spare, as the cost of one beverage is the admission price for a chair in a cafe and one is seldom pressurised into consuming more. Incidentally, in those places where they provide standing room at the counter, it will cost you considerably less than at the table. Bear this in mind if it is only a brief break and use of their washing facilities you need.

Un jour sans vin c'est un jour sans soleil is a French saying. A day without wine is a day without sun. I, too, find wine brings light into my life. This is the one thing which is very much cheaper in Latin countries — it is not merely cheaper it is just not expensive and non-vintage table wine costs substantially less than beer or soft-drinks. Unfortunately it is not a substitute for other beverages in the middle of the day. Don't drink and drive is a sound motto. Taken in moderation with a meal it is not likely to affect your judgement, but in hot weather don't touch it as it can cause drowsiness in the afternoon. I include these words of caution because its very cheapness makes it a temptation.

If you are campers and prepare most of your own meals and refreshments, by price awareness and cautious buying, you should be able to sustain yourself adequately for very little more than it costs you at home.

Never avoid stopping if you are tired or hungry. This is a typical French Autoroute cafeteria 'complex'

11 Don't follow your nose – look for the sun

Some years ago when we were heading down for Grenoble, a town at the foot of the French Alps, we came across a group of young riders whose British (GB) registered bikes were parked on our side of the road. Naturally, we stopped to talk to them and they seemed most concerned that they had still not picked up the Paris road signs after travelling since early morning. At first they were most unwilling to accept our assurance that though they were on the right road they were headed in the wrong direction! I then raised the point that Paris lay roughly to the north from the point where we were standing that early afternoon and after a confab among themselves they agreed that this was so.

"In which case, surely the sun should not be shining down almost directly in your eyes but should be behind you?" I put it as a question.

We watched the thought processes going on through their range of expressions which slowly gave way to dismay, as they were now about 400 miles distant from their intended night stop!

Most unjustly we were hated for it, but that is the way of people to those who bring them bad tidings.

This is the most extreme instance we have encountered, of people who have headed in the wrong direction for such a prolonged period of time, but on many other occasions we have redirected motorists who were sadly off course.

Humans are not highly endowed with instincts when they pop out into this world and certainly not with a sense of direction. The so called 'sense' is really based on acquired knowledge, learned largely from observation and experience – the experienced traveller is aware of the direction in which he is travelling by his relation to the sun at any time during the day, and is quickly alerted if it does not correspond to his destination.

On rainy days when there is a heavy, low cloud ceiling, which the sun totally fails to penetrate to give a brighter glow in one area, there are still other clues to indicate that you are following a fairly steady course. If the wind changes from your right side to the rear – or slow scudding cloud alters direction – be alert, as it is more likely to be you that has altered course rather than the wind. Trees in exposed areas have a permanent lean according to the prevailing wind. Houses standing on their own, particularly mansions, usually have their main aspect facing south.

Obviously being aware of the signs loses most of its significance on a motorway or well indicated main road but it is a very different matter once you are attracted onto the lesser byways. Since Mollie and I have adventurous natures, we will strike away cross country when we are not hard pressed for time, where many of the secondary roads lack adequate signs at intersections and junctions, or perhaps are not signed at all, as they are primarily used by the locals. We have made some very long journeys this way and Mollie, who is yet more observant than I am, has a highly developed sense and is able to cope with the inevitable variations in direction, since roads, nearly all of them, do not continue in a straight line but meander from side to side towards their objective.

She has a sort of inbuilt computer which tells her when we have been deviating too far to the right of a course, and that this must be countered by an equal leg to the left, as soon as we have the choice to do so. Consequently, we do not often lose our way, even over a confused country network and, if we do, it will not be long before we feel our way back to where we should be going.

As mentioned earlier, it is most important you should know the general compass bearing of your route.

Which way?

When was this photograph taken? Probably in the late summer (ricks in the background) and riders dressed as though it had been warm earlier on. (Length of shadow confirms late afternoon), travelling south

Maps are conveniently laid out from South to North, the South being towards you, the bottom edge or margin running from due West to East. The only exceptions to this rule I have encountered are in bound books of maps (an atlas) when, because of the limited space available, a country may be tilted relative to the compass — they will do this with Italy, for example, because of its shape. In this case they will indicate North with a prominent arrow — at least on those that I have seen.

   When studying a map on the road it is helpful to relate it to the compass so that North on the map is actually in a northerly direction. This way it is easier to orientate yourself; where the road is shown to curve left on the map, look up in the direction you are headed and it becomes more apparent. If you look at the map the wrong way up, relative to the direction you are pointed, it is not always obvious and, furthermore the sun will not be in the correct relationship to the map the way you are seeing it.

   I have not yet bothered with anything so scientific as one of those compasses that float in liquid and are suitable for installation on a motor vehicle. I imagine one might be useful at times, although you would probably have to come to a stop to read the thing accurately, and this will not tell you whether you are already off course and must bear left or right to achieve a correction. The best instrument for rapid calculation, able to deal with enforced deviations without having to distract your attention from the road and its traffic, is your head, but, like a computer, you must be alert to all the signs and symbols you feed into it for it to produce the right answer.

   I have mentioned that you do not need a developed sense of direction when you are on a motorway — but I must add — providing it is the right motorway! You do not have to be excessively dim to take the wrong one at a multiple interchange — I've done it! At least I became quickly aware of my mistake, without the help of a road-sign to tell me, and I did not go blithely rolling by the next exit for another forty miles.

TENEZ LA DROITE

   To help you with your French it translates literally "Hold the Right", in other words "Drive on the Right".
   In practice, most drivers quickly adapt themselves to driving on their unaccustomed side of the road and only for the first few miles are slightly confused about which way to look for approaching traffic at intersections. This certainly causes me no problem when I am in control of a vehicle though, oddly, I become hopeless as a pedestrian and I have heard from others that they are likewise affected. In countries where you drive on the right (and that is most of them) traffic approaches from the right and on dual carriageways (divided highways) the slow lane is on the right, as it is on the left in England.
   The main danger of which you must be aware is when you start out in the morning or after a stop, when it is all too easy to set off absent-mindedly on the wrong side of the road. Thus it helps to use a sticker in a prominent location where you will see it — it does not necessarily have to state 'Drive on the Right' an arrow will do, anything to call your attention to the requirement at the vital moment when you start out.
   By far the greatest danger is when you return back home when you are less keyed up to adapt to the change of sides. This was thought to be the cause of a fatal accident to a friend of mine. I don't believe in using scary examples to put a point across but this really happened, so I mention it. Since I travel a great deal of mileage abroad I have also been prone to make this mistake, usually when I have been back a few days, but fortunately I have always been suddenly alerted in time to correct the error, although I have not always avoided embarrassment. So now I make a point of reversing that sticker to remind me to keep left, on my return.

This is a typical compass which should provide accurate readings and prove to be robust enough for the job

The universal 'keep right' sign has particular significance in Europe!

H.6075

Bob Carpenter, Editor of *Road Rider,* sets off for his six or seven mile jog before breakfast

12 Early to bed and early to rise

So at last the tour has started and, for most, it will be in the long, (hopefully) hot days of summer. You won't be alone; some tens of thousands of others will have the same idea in whatever state, county or province you may be travelling. Start off early when the air is crisp and bright. Apart from localised commuter traffic, the roads will be relatively quiet as, on the holiday routes, the main build up is from about 9 am till noon but quietening down again from just before 1 o'clock till 2.30 in the afternoon, while people stop for lunch or picnic. Take advantage of the slack hours, when others are eating. Here I speak from experience as when I am keyed up on some test or press activity, I can actually be on the road by 6 am. The early riser has the advantage of being able to look round for accommodation by, say, 4 o'clock in the afternoon, which is a point to consider on main holiday routes or resorts as from early evening onwards, countless others will be doing just that and may over-flow the accommodation available.

When you take to the road at a late hour, the sparkle will be gone from the morning and you will spend a large part of the afternoon trying to make up for lost time, unless you have a very easy schedule. Here I can speak with far greater experience as, when I am not keyed up in a competitive spirit, I am destined by nature to be a dilatory riser who lacks co-ordination till well after breakfast. Here I am not alone and I feel I am too often unjustly blamed for having to accept a dismal room at a high price because we have left it till after dark. Many are the occasions too when we have pitched camp in the fading dusk, when the mosquitoes are out in hunting packs.

As will be seen from this, the advice which I ladle out is based on experience, not just the experience of doing all the right things but knowing full well the consequences of not being my own disciple. So if I say 'do' and you darned well don't want to, then my reply is 'that's up to you, mate. That makes two of us!' No, in reality, unless I confess otherwise I actually do follow my own preachings most of the time but I also speak from the experience of having made nearly all the mistakes in the book on some occasion or another.

PHYSICAL FITNESS

I have already made passing mention that you don't have to be an athlete to ride a motorcycle, but it helps. Differing from other forms of mechanical transport you are perched on your vehicle, not in it, and there is constant muscular activity going on, however slight, by rider and passenger, as they respond to the requirements of a two wheeled vehicle. A long run, particularly in inclement weather, calls for stamina and you'll soon begin to suffer if you are out of condition.

Lethargic I may be in the early hours but I have been endowed with a wiry frame and I have never had to struggle against obesity which becomes the enemy of so many with the passing years. Even so, I am not able to rely on continued resilience after a spell of inactivity, and included in my planning for a long journey is a course, however inadequate, of improving my physical fitness. So, some weeks before the event, I will start to work up to twenty push-ups first thing in the morning, touch toes without bending knees (that's the great achievement), bend, wave arms about, take deep breaths, then take the dog out for long walks, to his surprise and pleasure. Cut down on smokes — a filthy habit I ought to abandon entirely though lack the will power — take the bike over some rough terrain both for practice and to supple up the muscles. If it's going to be an arduous trip I will actually put quite a lot of energy into the toughening up process.

Finale.....Ken gets switched on with an electric powered trials bike

Take heed, you sedentary workers who never get your feet wet. Supple up before the event or your journey may be a painful trial instead of a pleasurable adventure.

It would not be encouraging advice on my part to suggest that you must be tough to undertake a tour by motorcycle. There are those who don't want to be, the very feminine lass who owns a little bike because it is the most economical means of transport — or the physically inadequate or even handicapped. They can set themselves an easy time schedule which will enable them to be fine weather riders most of the time. Yet even here they are displaying a spirit of adventure when there is nothing to prevent them staying at home and watching TV. My feeling is that almost anyone, apart from those with serious problems, will come to no harm by over-stretching themselves and suffering discomfort and privation at times. I will be more positive than that, for Mollie and I have undertaken assignments that involved physical strain, shortage of sleep and even inadequate nourishment and have come back looking gaunt and in need of a short period of recuperation. Yet, in the long term, I think we are tougher and more durable for these experiences. Life is for living, not decaying, and accepting a challenge and overcoming the hardships is a good thing for the body and, not least, one's morale.

So it's night and raining; visibility is poor, you are cold and damp despite wearing the right clothing, and it's going to be all of thirty miles before you can expect to find shelter. Take heart, you'll survive if you started out in good shape and, what could be better, you will benefit from the experience!

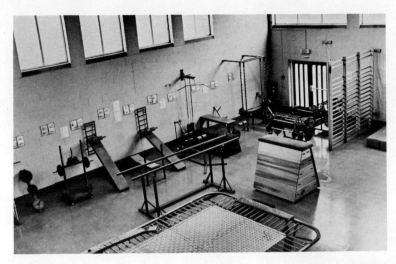

Even if you don't have facilities like these, being especially fit will help you enjoy your motorcycle touring

There are many methods for learning languages. This is one of the more popular record programmes

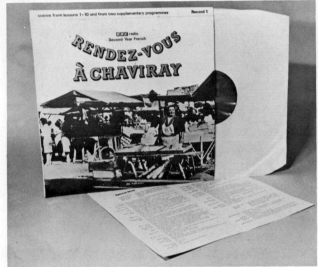

LANGUAGES

Have a bash!

I am not referring to the four letter, old Anglo Saxon variety, but while on this aspect it is useful to be equipped with a good vocabulary and the ability to devise ingenious combinations — providing you hold them in reserve for really dire circumstances when you can vent your rage at fate rather than your wife or travel companions.

Actually I allude to the ineptitude of the average Britisher at coping with a foreign language and I consider we are rivalled only by Americans in our resistance to learning the tongues of those other barbarians who are unable to speak English.

When you think of it, the motives for wanting to explore beyond your own secure surroundings are for change, farmer families enjoy a spree in town, folk from the mountains make their way to the sea. In Europe you don't have to spread your tentacles very far to be among people who speak a different language. If you are merely English speaking, don't let the prospect worry you. There will be a great many 'foreigners' in the places you visit, who will speak our language because we have been too darned lazy to learn theirs. Furthermore, these foreigners are generally less inhibited about conveying messages in sign language and the latins in particular are more prone to use hands, arms and facial expression to emphasise or give extra definition to their spoken words. So don't worry about making a game of it — it will usually be accepted with patience and good humour. Snags can arise, however, about more technical things such as trying to persuade an attendant at the filling station that the oil for your four stroke motorcycle is not put in the same place as the petrol. Of this beware, it has happened to a lot of people — once to me when my attention was distracted. Eating can be a problem too, if you go where the locals go and not where they cater for tourists. In our travels through the remoter Balkans we became fed up — in the literal sense too — with never ending goulash. Our problem there was that the written language was in Cyrillic and we have lacked the ambition to learn a fresh alphabet.

Be prepared for bad weather. This competitor in the Scottish 6 Days Trial doesn't look too happy

When Mollie and I started our adventures together we had the advantage of an extra language each, not the same one. From the start we became highly competitive in acquiring basic vocabularies through the other countries we visited. We are about neck and neck in the number of ways we are able to say 'thank you' a most useful word which, in isolation, can win you friends. **Yes** and **No** are easy to master, also **loo (bathroom** to you Americans who are afraid to call a spade a spade), **good, sleep, bedroom, eat, food, drink, water, please, the numerals, how much** (relating to cost). I give these as a basic vocabulary which will take you a long way combined with gestures to fill in the verbs. The numerals are probably less vital for a start and take longer to learn — after all, you have your fingers. Most helpful are the pleasantries, the salutations, and the greetings of the country, **please, good morning, good night,** etc. How long will it take you to learn twenty words?....have a bash!

I grant there is plenty of scope for misunderstandings but these usually add to the jollity of the occasion such as when the young batchelor becomes the reluctant host of the plump, middle aged receptionist. When this happens be gallant and demonstrate your linguistic ability with 'Vive le sport!'

Naturally it is helpful to start off with a smattering — one can get this by following the language courses on BBC television, or evening classes or records. Is this carrying preparations for a trip abroad too far? Of course, the crazy thing is that nearly every Britisher has had French as a compulsory school subject but what tiny bit was ever absorbed is soon discarded. It is when you go to a country that it acquires a real meaning, it becomes the real live thing which ought to provide an incentive. Don't regard it just as homework for a fleeting visit - regard it as a start to greater things. After all, we are now living in each others pockets.

13 Roadcraft

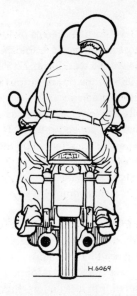

H.6069

MOUNTAINS

To the Englishman at least, snowcapped mountains should be a 'must' at least once in a lifetime. The Pyrenees reach almost from coast to coast, along each side of the French/Spanish frontier, the great Alpine range extends from Southwest France through parts of Switzerland, Italy, Germany, and Austria before finally tapering down in Yugoslavia. So whether you head southwest or southeast from the channel ports, there will generally be mountains that straddle some of the direction of your travels if followed in a straight line. Incredibly (to me) in these days of main road mania, the majority of motoring tourists from all of northern or central Europe will choose a route which outflanks them, or goes through by tunnel. Crossing mountains is no joy in wet weather so if the forecast is for continuing rain or if you are already in it when approaching a mountainous area, you are free to switch to the lower routes that lead to the Mediterranean and here you will benefit from having an open itinerary, having previously worked on the alternatives available. But if the sun shines down warmly and the sky looks good, make the most of it and involve yourself in some high pass bashing for real motorcycling pleasure.

This does not, as some people imagine, call for superlative riding skill, unless one's machine happens to be so much of a roadburning type that it becomes unmanageable when trying to drop below 30 mph to negotiate a bend. Mountain roads, as built for modern traffic, follow a zig zag course. A short straight (or nearly straight) section of quite modest gradient, leads to a bend which probably completes a full switchback of 360 degrees, followed by another short straight, and so on, all the way up, and all the way down. An adaptable rider can soon acquire bend swinging techniques, selecting the right gear in advance to change up and round the bends, or to retard when going down — it is a great way to improve your riding skill.

Strangely, quite a lot of people suffer from vertigo, particularly the passengers; and this can rather detract from the pleasure. Of course, there are hazards but it is the unforeseen ones that cause most of the mishaps and accidents in this world. On mountains the danger is all too visible: it is that terrifying drop on one side of the road (which for half the time will be on your side) and seldom in these circumstances will there be railings to prevent you from taking off down a near vertical precipice. This imposes its own discipline! But in truth it does not add one whit to the danger. True, if you do run off the road and drop down a few hundred feet or a thousand — it makes no odds — you are not very likely to feel the pain! Equally, on the ordinary familiar main road, if you run off it at 40 mph directly into a brick wall or buildings that line it, or into the back of a sand lorry, this is likely to be pretty fatal too. People do run out of road from time to time from inattention or over confidence. This is more likely where there is no apparent hazard and, if lucky, they get away with nothing worse than a shaking up. Few, if any, touring riders will behave in an overfamiliar way with mountain roads and, in fact, accidents on the precipitous sections are rare in the extreme.

I would go so far as to say that high mountain roads are almost certainly the safest for the very reason that drivers dare not take chances. Any natural anxiety about precipices can often be allayed by the way one thinks of things. Not "what if I fall off" but rather "so long as I stay on the road I am safe". This is merely something you have been doing all your motorcycling life (I hope) so what is all the fuss about?

An aspect to riding in the mountains that is generally overlooked is that as you ascend the air becomes thinner and engine power decreases at roughly 3% per thousand feet altitude, maximum power, or 100%, being achieved at sea level for the average piston engine without supercharger. This decline in power will not be noticed with most motorcycles as the change is very gradual, but there are quite a few passes of over 7,000 feet when the engine will be working at 77.5% of maximum efficiency. If you go over the highest pass in Europe, Col d'Iseran, 9,085 ft. the power output will be down to about 70% and a pipsqueak might be in some difficulties on steep gradients.

Water boils at a lower temperature with increasing altitude and it is nigh impossible to make a drinkable brew of tea when you are above 5,000 ft.

Very few people are affected by mountain sickness but it can be very serious for those so afflicted. It happens to folk who cannot adapt to the change in atmospheric pressure and the symptom is vomiting, followed by frequent spells of retching. The only cure is to descend again and this should be done without delay. As mentioned, this is a rare complaint so don't let it put you off having a run over high mountains.

TECHNIQUES FOR COPING WITH THE ROUGH, THE SLIPPERY AND FLOODS

In the early days when I was persuading my wife that a motorcycle was our perfect means of transport, she was greatly influenced by my salesmanship of the wonderful, tractable ability of the two wheeler, which would go anywhere a mule could find a footing. Taking me at my word, she directed me to the most outlandish places and I was projected into learning the hard way about rough riding, through self-experience. After traversing a few thousand miles on byways in the Balkans, and dropping the bike a couple of times together with my passenger, I began to acknowledge that techniques are not necessarily best acquired through self-tuition and, in fact, one can go about things in the wrong way, forming bad habits that can be hard to shed. This, to my satisfaction, I confirmed after taking a one-day course as a pupil of Hugh Viney, the great trials champion of the early 1950s. This does not make me an expert, I could never be that, but I think I can pass on some useful tips which are still valid today, despite the passage of time. At this stage my audience may say that they have no intention of riding up a river bed in Macedonia because it is in a better state than the main road. Maybe they don't want to go to Macedonia and, in any case, the roads will have improved since then. Ah! but would you go out in a boat with a fine weather yachtsman who was not interested in the actions required in the event of a storm? It is not as though you will always have a choice of the highway conditions you tackle other than by abandoning the steed when things become sticky and hitchhiking the rest of the way. The Continentals, particularly the French, take a military approach to resurfacing their roads and great clanking machines strip off the whole lot, not just one lane at a time. The next stage is to spread loose chippings or worse for a temporary thoroughway, and this can go on for miles. Many of the higher mountain roads are churned up by the spring thaw and it can take most of the summer season to clear off the mud and fill in the water courses. Coping with the hazards is all part of the game.

The first unnerving experience to confront the novice is to run unexpectedly onto a ball bearing surface which is the description given to small stones which remain spread on a road after resurfacing. One's first reaction is to hang on tight and pray. Prayer may help the devout, hanging on tight will not. In reality, the feeling that the bike is going out of control is more psychological than real, but there is an element of danger if you do the wrong things. On a shifting surface relax, or at least pretend to relax, even if you can't. Keep your feet on the pegs and don't grip the bars as if you are in a state of rigor mortis. Let the bike take its head within limitations as its natural tendency will be to drift and weave slightly. There will be a human desire to slow down but the expert will keep driving ahead and will finally accelerate out of trouble, once he has seen the end of the loose section. If you must slow down because of a curve or trouble ahead, try to do so only through the gears and if you must brake you should resort to quick dabs on-and-off, to avoid the possibility of a wheel locking. Although a front wheel slide will almost certainly bring you off, the front brake is still the most effective, but use it with the tips of your fingers.

The techniques for riding on slippery roads, mud, snow and ice are similar, but at all costs avoid getting caught out at high speed as subsequent slowing down requires a long distance. I am told there is nothing quite as slippery as petrol on a smooth road, so take it very easy if you pass a scene of a recent accident, particularly if there is a tanker on its side. It may seem far-fetched that I should mention anything so remote but it was just such a happening that brought down a cluster of riders on a Partitour, though fortunately without serious damage. Viney's suggestion for riding over snow and ice is to reduce tyre pressures to a little above half the recommended pressure — not forgetting to re-inflate for normal conditions. When I put this recommendation into print for the first time, its merit was subsequently disputed in the correspondence columns of the journal. But to me it makes sense and I stand fast to it.

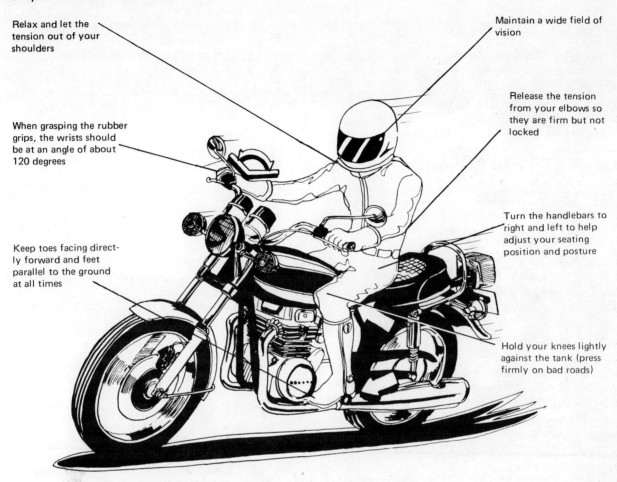

Relax and let the tension out of your shoulders

Maintain a wide field of vision

When grasping the rubber grips, the wrists should be at an angle of about 120 degrees

Release the tension from your elbows so they are firm but not locked

Keep toes facing directly forward and feet parallel to the ground at all times

Turn the handlebars to right and left to help adjust your seating position and posture

Hold your knees lightly against the tank (press firmly on bad roads)

This illustrates what might be described as 'good riding form'. Read the individual captions

This is what happens when an excess of front brake is applied (*left*), and rear brake (*right*). Again read the individual captions

Front wheel brake action:
When you apply the front brake only the centre of gravity moves toward the front wheel — especially on corners or slippery surfaces

Rear wheel brake action:
When braking from high speeds, the rear wheel tends to lose some traction on the road surface and making it prone to locking. Forceful application of the rear wheel brake alone should be avoided at high speeds

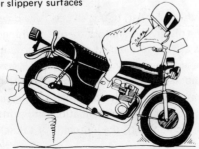

Although, of course, taken during a trials riding competition, Y. Vesterinen illustrates the style needed for a really loose surface even on a touring motorcycle

Banking:
Rider and motorcycle bank at the same angle for stability, manoeuverability and better perception at corners.

Lean in:
The rider leans inward while the angle of the motorcycle is kept moderate. This posture is recommended for wet and slippery road conditions.

Lean out:
The rider's body is raised above the angle of the motorcycle. This form allows for maximum banking angles and better control on poor road surfaces

Three types of cornering technique, each one having its particular use and advantage

Rough riding in Arizona

Actually you are not likely to do much damage merely by coming off at slow speed in such circumstances, as the bike will lay down most gracefully in a slide on ice. It is the following traffic that is the peril and the average motorist who lacks two wheel experience will be unaware that he will be unable to stop within a short distance. Here, again, I am referring to glazed ice, which does not look menacing from the inside of a warm saloon. Another peril which is easily overlooked is rain after a long dry spell, which can create ice-like conditions when it wets an accumulated deposit of rubber and oil on the road surface.

The only advantage to dragging your feet under slippery conditions is that it tells the fellow behind that adhesion is poor and that you are scared to death! In fact, putting the feet down is no aid at all to keeping upright; on the contrary, it detracts from control. Go slowly yes, but not so slowly you have to jiggle the front wheel to maintain balance. Snow is not too bad, even when packed. For one thing it is self-proclaiming to the motorist behind and it is usually possible to pick one's way, avoiding the glossiest patches. Control the bike delicately with the tips of fingers. Just relax! Well, try to.

Floods can catch you out unexpectedly — and certainly will in the course of time, no less in an urban area after that sudden cloudburst and a blocked outlet to a drain. With the sun out again and a rainbow across a receding storm cloud, that mud coloured pond at the dip in the road looks easy enough to cross. It probably is, but go into it slowly or the resultant backwash may do dire things to your electrics and remember to drive for a short distance after emerging with your brakes applied until they bite — particularly drum brakes. But one may be

It's not always summer in the mountains. This shot was taken in the Grossglockner during a summer Partitour

faced with deeper water for a longer distance and it may be advisable to pause for a moment before attempting the crossing. How deep is it likely to be? — even without the guide of other traffic going through there are usually ways of assessing this by gates, hedges, roadsigns. You must consider the prospect of being lost halfway across if there is an absence of navigational signs — and don't think this is impossible because it happened to me in a valley in Yugoslavia, when Mollie had to dismount and feel her way along the road as I followed. If the bike has low level silencers which become submerged, you must keep the throttle well open to overcome the back pressure and keep your speed down by letting the clutch slip, which is a bad practice under any other circumstance. Don't let the engine stall if you can possibly avoid it. It is unlikely you would be able to restart and worse, the engine is prone to kick back where there is back pressure when it could feasibly suck in enough water to blow the top off. If there is flood water streaming across a gulley, it is advisable to wade in and investigate whether rocks or boulders have been washed onto the surface. Whatever else don't drop your bike in the water — where there are rocks drive with your feet down — not just drag them but good purposeful strides keeping as close to the vertical as possible by muscle power rather than by balance. Drastic situations call for drastic measures. Mollie and I were once marooned in an industrial suburb of Genova for two days. If I had had the confidence and knowledge I gained later with Viney this would not have happened. We would have driven over that bridge before the water was halfway up the parapet.

Riding in the mountains can sometimes be tantamount to riding in the rough because of the road surface

Hugh Viney, trials ace, who taught so many of today's experts how to ride on the rough. They don't make caps like that any more!

I am not able to give any useful guidance in a short space about coping with the unmade mountain trail of large stones and slabs of rock or the impetus and throttle opening you'll need to surmount a 1 in 3 rise over a shale surface. It is a feature of most modern motorcycles that they rely on a fist full of revs. for their power and lack torque lower down the scale, which imposes limitations. Desirably, you should learn the limitations of the bike and yourself as a rider by practicing when the steed is unladen so it is less of a handful when you find yourself in trouble. I certainly do not wish to give the impression that one should be a cross-country expert before setting out on a tour. Very few people are, because they have never bothered, but how helpful it might be to know and what fun to find out the extent of one's ability and one's nerve. Of course, people are reluctant to risk dropping an expensive glossy steed trying out their skill over obstacles, but it is a question of what one attempts. Start off with the relatively simple and work up. Incidentally, I have not yet damaged myself or a bike when parting company at low speed, when I have been prepared for it to happen, but with heavy models it is desirable to have someone standing by to do some weight lifting, if required. Inevitably, there are some risks if you set out deliberately to tackle difficult terrain and I must now disclaim responsibility for any dented models or sprained ankles which are consequent on my suggestion that you have a go. Yet the developing of skill is not only fun but a challenge and equips one to deal with the greater hazard, of being caught out untrained and lacking practice when unavoidable difficulties arise in the course of a journey which are not of your own choice of timing.

14 Road sense –survival

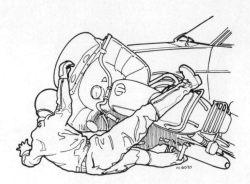

Suggest to a driver (or rider) that his road sense is perhaps not quite so good as it might be and the chances are that you have made an enemy for life. Yet how can you explain a way round about 7,500 deaths on the road each year in this country alone! There is little consolation in the fact that our record is better, relative to the number of vehicles, than most of the rest of the world — in which the total carnage amounts to a dreadful quarter of a million.

How can so-called sane people accept such a figure with equanimity? And since all but a small percentage can be attributed to simple acts of misjudgement, therefore it follows that almost all are avoidable. This, of course, is an over-simplification, since it fails to take into account that humans are not infallible. On the other hand the incidence could be enormously reduced through better training and, above all, a much more self-critical attitude.

And who am I to set myself up as an authority — it being the way of drivers not to accept that someone may know more about driving than they do? Furthermore, I've not been all that clever either and I have a few mended bones to show for it (even though it was a long while ago). So, never being too late to learn, I hit on the idea of visiting the Motor Driving School of the Metropolitan Police Force since they collectively must know most of what is to be known on survival in dangerous conditions. Scotland Yard were not averse to the idea but sticky at first, wanting to know more about me and the publication envisaged. This was fair enough for when they co-operate they do it well, involving some expense and taking up the time of quite a number of officers.

After I had been made welcome at the Driving School, an Inspector was the first to take me in hand. "I'll start off as though you were a new recruit into the motorcycle section and summarise some of the important aspects of their first lectures."

"Get it right out of your head that there is such a thing as a born driver — or rider. They don't exist. Man is among the slowest moving and most ponderous of animals and his inborn reflexes are equally slow. He can't match a cat for speed and reaction, nor a dog before it is overfed. Most of the herd animals run much faster than we can, and then change course in a flash and never collide with each other. As an extreme example, think of the swallow which weaves and zips about, catching insects on the wing. We're lame dinosaurs by comparison. Motor vehicles have not existed long enough to develop a new breed of man with the instinctive reactions and judgement needed to cope with the speeds at which we can now project ourselves. The point I am trying to emphasize is that you are not endowed by nature to drive a motor vehicle and you have to learn every inch of the way.

"Now the learning process started when you first focused on traffic from your pram and even more when Dad drove you about in the car. The first time you take over the control of a powered vehicle you have already had experience. If Pop was an 'amber gambler' — a traffic light jumper — you will have been preconditioned into being one too. So from our first driving lesson the probability is that you have a fair amount to unlearn as well as learn. The first essential in becoming an expert is to be self-critical and aware of one's own inadequacies and by the time you are an expert you will be even more aware of your own imperfections. Now for a demonstration".

I was taken into a room in which was the apparatus for a simulated brake test and I was placed in the driving seat of a mock-up car. Ahead of me was a screen on which was projected a typical urban traffic scene. I now pressed the accelerator so that the speedometer needle registered 30 mph when suddenly the images on the screen altered to a dangerous situation. I then had to demonstrate how long it took me to transfer my foot to the

Ken riding at the Police Motorcycle Training School

brake pedal and apply pressure. This was accurately registered on a large dial, .425 secs.

"That's better than average," announced the Inspector. "But in that time you covered 18.7 ft. and to bring your vehicle to a halt would have taken another 45 ft. when braking on a dry surface. Your reaction time was when you were all keyed up to act promptly — it would probably have taken twice as long under normal circumstances; if this had been so you would have covered more than 37 ft before you even started to brake. This is where a little scientific knowledge will help counteract human imperfection — you will make allowances for the lag and adjust your speed accordingly. An understanding of braking distance is the absolute first essential in safe vehicle control and to know how to brake....!

"The first practical lesson on a machine for our coppers is a prolonged series of braking tests. As you will be aware, in a crash stop situation the natural tendency is to stamp on everything and when this happens the back wheel locks, when it not only loses most of its efficiency to retard but sends the bike slewing from side to side with the prospect that the rider will be thrown. On wet roads the front brake can also lock and if this happens the bike will promptly lie down. Nevertheless, the front brake is the best stopper. On comparative testing the retardation efficiency is 75 — 25, on a dry surface between front and rear wheel and about 50 — 50 when it's wet. Obviously the best result is achieved by applying both to maximum pressure, up to the point they are about to lock but not beyond. This takes more practice than any other aspect of bike control so that the rider responds to training and does not panic in crash situations. And having said all this, the emphasis on the rest of the course is to prevent situations arising which call for panic stops."

The RAC-ACU Training Scheme provides a very good but cheap means of learning to ride safely. Many towns throughout Britain have a local scheme in operation.

Bruce Preston, editor of *Motorcycle Rider,* remains a safe distance behind a car turning to the right

Grouping of controls is important. They should operate easily so that there is no chance of inadvertent use in an emergency situation

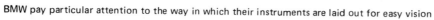

BMW pay particular attention to the way in which their instruments are laid out for easy vision

Next I was taken to a class in progress, where trainees were gathered round engines and gearboxes which were cut away to expose the moving parts, as well as some beautiful working models produced in the Police workshops. It was then explained to me that all Police riders underwent a basic course in motorcycle mechanics, not because they were expected to service their machines but for what is called 'machine sympathy.' The contention being that a rider becomes more proficient when he knows what is going on underneath.

There was just enough time in the morning for me to be pressed into giving a demonstration obstacle ride through and about markers round which I had to perform some very sharp turns as well as show fine judgement. After doing a certain amount of foot dabbing — which I blamed on the high revving Honda 4 — I received a left-handed compliment from the Sergeant instructor. "Well, I will say you did darned well — for a beginner."

He went on, "I'd like to see you have a bash at our scrambles course. That's not here; we go out to the army range for that. That's really tough and we keep piling on the misery until even the best rider comes adrift at least once, just to let him know he is not yet perfect! Yes, I know, they have only to ride in the metropolitan area on their job but if they are expert at something difficult, they will be better experts at the more simple. Come on, it's time you went for lunch."

We had a wide ranging discussion over the dining table with myself posing the questions to an authoritative group from the traffic division and a man from Scotland Yard. From this emerged that police motorcycles were involved in less accidents than police cars relative to miles covered, which would indicate that the motorcycle is not inherently the most dangerous vehicle. "But the people who ride them are" came like a chorus from several mouths at the same time.

Regrettably, the ratio of accidents swings drastically the other way among civilian riders and of these a disproportionately high figure, again relative to numbers, was among first year riders. It was not so much that they lacked skill as road sense. In fact, it was the opinion that the real danger period was when a rider had achieved a fair degree of technical expertise, and confidence, or over confidence, rushes ahead of experience or a real understanding of the dangers.

The major contributory cause to accidents involving motorcyclists in urban areas is that the motorcyclists are insufficiently visible. Hence the recommendation that the riders should wear bright colours, although this will cope with only part of the problem. Motorcyclists who have not themselves driven cars fail to appreciate that virtually all have blind spots when approached from the rear and, in any case, drivers can only give cursory glances at their wing mirrors when having to cope with constantly varying traffic situations around them. Overtaking on the inside between traffic and the kerb or between two lines of traffic moving in the same direction is a danger-ous procedure. Even when traffic is stationary, doors can be suddenly swung open by a passenger who decides to step out and this is not an infrequent happening. An experienced motorcyclist is always aware that he and his machine occupy a very small area and is alert to the fact that he may not have been seen. And then, of course, there is the old, old story of riding too fast in relation to conditions. Bikes, by their nature, want to get up and go and it requires restraint not to ride at 25 mph when a sane speed would be 18. You can do yourself a lot of damage hitting something at 25 mph or, as is the case, 37 ft. per second.

"Yes, but surely there are times when you must accelerate out of trouble rather than brake into it" I said.

The Inspector gave me a severe look "That's a dangerous philosophy to preach. You use the word 'trouble' to indicate an awkward situation in which you find yourself unexpectedly. And this should never arise."

"There but for the grace of God go I" I muttered.

The Inspector smiled and went on. "Of course you use acceleration in preference to braking quite a lot of the time but it's something you have calculated on in advance. The rider must look well ahead and plan his course of action by taking into account all other moving things which can be pedestrians and dogs as well as other traffic. It's all a bit of a chess game played at the double. You must calculate your own movement according to the anticipated movements of others but since people are capable of doing the unexpected you must also have considered your options. But calculations of this sort require knowledge, knowledge which is largely based on one's own observations and experience, since the permutations are almost endless and cannot all be taught in the classroom, let alone memorised. So back we come to the danger period of the young. Let's take a way-out example; the young fellow who is beginning to make his mark at racing. How are you going to convince him he is still a novice in urban traffic and that he needs more experience before he starts dicing? He'll probably rely on his powerful bike and split second reactions to zoom him out of danger. But he's likely to come unstuck on the occasion he is very much below par and no man should ever rely on his judgement or reactions being wholly consistent. That's another sign of being a mature driver — he will know when he is tired or otherwise below form and modulate his pace accordingly."

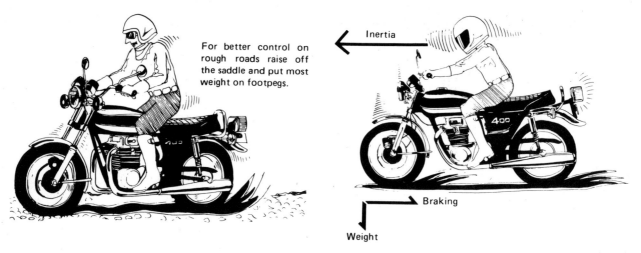

For better control on rough roads raise off the saddle and put most weight on footpegs.

This is a fundemental riding technique for better control over slippery bumpy or flooded surfaces. Raise the body off the seat and put most of the weight on the foot rests *(left)*. The centre of gravity changes when accelerating relative to it when decelerating *(right)*

Different road surfaces give differing degress of traction

$$\text{Traction coefficient} = \frac{\text{Traction power}}{\text{Load (weight)}}$$

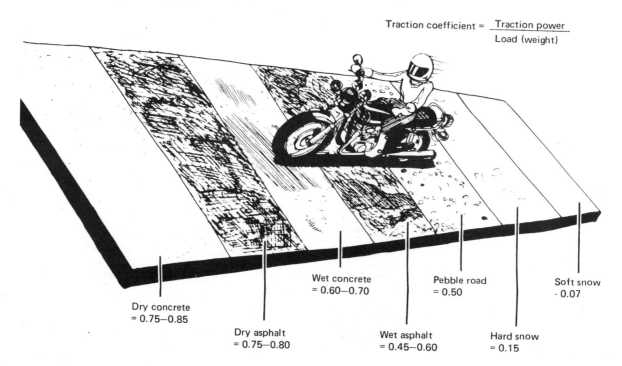

Dry concrete = 0.75—0.85

Dry asphalt = 0.75—0.80

Wet concrete = 0.60—0.70

Wet asphalt = 0.45—0.60

Pebble road = 0.50

Hard snow = 0.15

Soft snow - 0.07

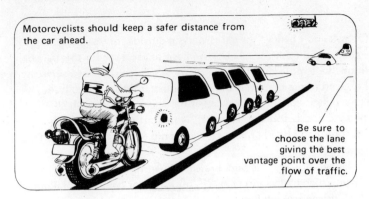

Motorcyclists should keep a safer distance from the car ahead.

Be sure to choose the lane giving the best vantage point over the flow of traffic.

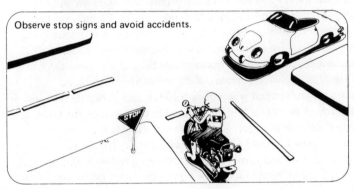

Observe stop signs and avoid accidents.

These four illustrations with their individual captions give an excellent coverage of the hazards to be encountered in town riding, and even on the open road

Ride defensively.

Try to anticipate hazards. People coming from behind parked cars may not notice you. Always be prepared for the unexpected.

At this point the Super. broke in,

"We have organised a commentary drive for you and I believe the car is waiting outside for you now."

The Sergeant Instructor from the Motorcycle Section took the wheel, "We have to use a car for this part of the course but bear in mind that I continue to think like a motorcyclist, particularly with regard to road surfaces. When I walked round the car before getting in I glanced to see that everything was intact, mirrors clean, tyres looked right and valve caps in place. If it had been a bike I would have glanced at the chain, even though all vehicles are checked and cleared by the service department, before handing over. Now start engine, check all lights are functioning, move forward slowly and test foot and hand brakes. How long did all this take?....seconds only but it's all part of a drill that makes sense."

"I am now going to give a commentary on planned driving," he said, pressing down firmly on the accelerator, and off we set. "Road ahead narrows with high hedges either side — mirror, clear behind — braking down to a safe speed and keeping watch on gardens, driveways and junctions for pedestrians, children and dogs. Now approaching a wider section of road with left hand bend — mirror, clear behind — taking a course on the crown of the road for better vision, speed too high, mirror still clear behind and brake down to a safe speed — gear too high — take second — accelerate away and up into third gear as the road straightens, road surfaces ahead changes, much smoother and not so good for braking and acceleration — mirror, clear behind - course is right, speed is right and as I am in third gear the gear is right. Approaching uncontrolled pedestrian crossing, no pedestrians — mirror, clear behind - course of approach correct but will reduce speed in case pedestrians appear — mirror clear, gently brake my speed down, I am already in third gear and will remain in third — over the crossing and accelerate away. Now a good straight road ahead and into top gear. Roundabout ahead when I intend to turn left — mirror, car good way behind, my course is correct in the nearside but will give left trafficator and reduce speed on the brakes to about 15 mph select second for the turn — mirror, still being followed but not too close, no pedestrians about, horn not required, heavy lorry coming in from the right, now clear, gentle acceleration on the turn, firmer as the vehicle straightens up and up into top gear as my speed increases."

"It's funny, you know," he turned to me when we were stopped at a light. "When a new recruit takes over on a commentary drive he'll be alright for a while until a whole cluster of signs catch up on him and he'll go slower and slower until he almost stops to find time to fit in all his observations. This is an indication he has not been looking far enough ahead or has been driving too fast in the first place. So we tell him that every time he gets on his bike he must carry on a running conversation with himself until it becomes an instilled habit."

"So next time a motorcycle copper comes to a stop alongside me at a traffic light talking out loud to no-one in particular...." I added, the Sergeant laughed as I hoped he would, even if it was only out of politeness.

We carried on the conversation in the canteen over pale cups of tea (don't think me ungrateful — on the contrary, I'm trying to improve the policeman's lot).

"I like to think of our fellows as being among the best trained in the world" His tone of voice made it sound modest. "Most other city forces will aim for the same things but I doubt if there are any others who can improve on our statistics. Our chaps operate in a high risk area and as you'll have seen for yourself they can turn up the wicks when an emergency call goes out on the air. Yet serious injuries are rare and I have to look back a lot of years to remember the last fatal. The secret, if it's a secret at all, is that our men have learned to ride over surfaces and conditions which are far worse than they will ever meet in real life.

"They must conduct themselves by the book which means that they will look expert and none of this unnecessary zip-bang stuff which is the sign of the immature private rider. By being part of an elite group of motorcyclists they can't kid their colleagues, and certainly not themselves, that they are God's chosen motorcyclist. Yet we want them to feel expert, remembering that an expert will never rest fully satisfied with his own performance. The safe rider is one who is constantly self-critical.

"I'm sorry" he went on "I must appear to be spouting from the introduction of a driving manual but it doesn't make it any the less true. The sad thing is that there is really no need for young motorcyclists to eliminate themselves the way they do. There are the R.A.C. — A.C.U. training schemes available for the novice — and a few of those who have already passed their driving test could do with some sessions too. Okay, they can't be anywhere near as thorough as police training and the average fellow doesn't get anything like the same amount of experience, but a training scheme does teach you to look at yourself so you'll never be satisfied, and that's four fifths of the way to being a safe rider."

Thank you, Scotland Yard and officers of the Metropolitan Police Driving School. If it has saved a few legs and just one life (though we'll never know) your help and time will all have proved worthwhile.

Safe journey!

15 Rules of the road

H.6067

Since every country has its own variations to driving rules and customs it is not possible to list them individually, nor could they possibly be remembered, but with so much intercontinental traffic on the roads a good deal of tolerance is extended to visitors and it is rare for a foreigner to be penalised for a minor infringement which he could not reasonably be expected to know, even though ignorance of the law is no excuse. Accordingly, I will confine this section to the general but bear in mind there will be exceptions. Just ride reasonably, particularly do not draw attention to yourself by brash behaviour as in many countries you can be fined on the spot on the uncorroborated judgement of a single policeman (not altogether unjustly; this happened to me in an Italian town, though I was honest enough to confess my speed). Keep your eyes alert to road signs which are now standard throughout most countries, apart from a few additions which some places still retain, though the pictorial messages they convey are usually easy enough to understand.

Drive on the right, remembering that the slow traffic lane is on the right. Overtake on the left. **Give way to** traffic approaching from the **right.**

Except to traffic on major highways in open country, no Frenchman will ever give way to vehicles on his left, even if it kills him, and despite any mandatory sign which might instruct him to do so. Other countries, in varying degrees and generally less lethal, follow the same code.

SPEED LIMITS — In General

60 kph (32½ mph) through towns, usually indicated by signs on entry. Ordinary highways (single carriageways) 100 kph (62½ mph). Motorways and most dual carriageways 130 kph (82 mph). No limit is imposed on the German autobahn.

Probably to a greater extent than in Britain, speed limits are largely ignored. In towns, for your own protection, it is advised to keep to the speed of the traffic stream. On the open roads you can also judge what is acceptable to the law enforcement people by the speed of the faster vehicles, but beware of radar traps on French motorways. 75 mph is adequate enough, except for humans with Superbikes, when an occasional blast off to brush aside the cobwebs is morally defensible when conditions are safe.

Take care turning left or right where there are traffic lights. You must give way to pedestrians crossing the road into which you have turned.

Headlights in France. France requires that motorcycles should be ridden with headlights on dipped beam during daylight. This applies to all places but I noted that French motorcyclists seem to ignore this requirement in the towns but not in the country. I imagine you will be safe in doing what they are doing but don't go by the mopeds, which are not regarded in the same category.

SPAIN

Motorists (including motorcyclists) involved in accidents in Spain are liable to find themselves popped into clink and questions asked afterwards. To avoid this prospect you are advised to take out a bail bond, which can be supplied by your insurers for a modest sum, or they can be obtained at the frontier.

The hand signal for turning right is to raise the left arm in the "teacher, may I leave the room" position. Directional indicators make this superfluous but you will know what is meant when Spanish riders do this. It is

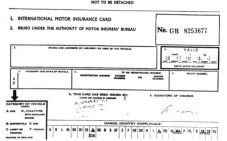

This is a typical Green Card; not an essential requirement for EEC countries but a wise one. It is necessary for other countries

It makes most sense to obtain a full passport, rather than a temporary one, if you are going well into Europe. Visas and border stamps are not necessary or that plentiful in Western Europe

not permitted to use dipped headlights in Spanish towns — pilot light only — at any time. In theory you are supposed to use horn or headlight before overtaking, but it is a requirement which is largely overlooked (thank goodness or it would be bedlam) but do not hesitate to do so with trucks. Spanish truck drivers are very helpful and will indicate with their nearside winkers or a green light when they consider it safe for you to overtake.

In general Continentals drive with more elan than in Britain. You'll soon get used to it and for your own survival 'when in Rome do as the Romans do.' This extra verve is much praised by the professional motoring and motorcycling journalists who confuse it with greater skill. This could be, but I deplore the incitement for the British to follow suit en masse on our highways, as they pay a heavier price than we do in terms of deaths and injuries.

Parking Most towns have special free parking sections for motorcycles which are easily spotted. Otherwise use your common sense avoiding the 'no parking' signs. In many towns parking alternates from one side of the road to the other, depending on the day of the week, so park on the side where other vehicles are parked.

Requirements for driving aboard A GB plate — a small one is legal for motorcycles — must be affixed at the rear of the vehicle, also a valid UK driving licence (not a provisional). Spain is the only country in Western Europe that requires an International Driving Permit, available through the RAC and AA (Actually I have never been asked yet to produce one but it will arise if you fall foul of the law). The vehicle log book. Insurance — your own insurance (take the Certificate) will give you limited cover in all the EEC countries and Austria, Finland, Norway, Sweden and Switzerland, but it will be third party indemnity only. You should notify your Insurers before departure. You are strongly advised however to obtain full cover, as afforded by a Green Card. Third Party (indemnity) insurance is required by all countries, and at others insurance cover can be obtained at main frontier crossings, for a fee. This can be troublesome, particularly if the appropriate office happens to be closed for one of many reasons. In any case, it is delaying. All countries require that a motorcycle is fitted with a rear view mirror. Protective helmets are mandatory in countries other than Italy and Spain.

The Green Card (It is actually printed on paper). Provides the same full cover as your normal one and is obtainable through your own insurers and is the immediate passport (together with the Log Book, not often asked for) for your vehicle abroad. The additional fee for this varies widely from one company to another and if you travel a lot it is worthwhile shopping around for the company that charges the least for this document as, in any case, it is quite expensive. It is advisable to apply to your insurers well in advance of your projected journey although normally they will, with some grumbling, issue you with one over the counter in the event of your making a snap decision — but telephone their office first.

Passport You must have a passport for travel abroad and you will be asked for it at the point of departure. These are available from any Crown (main) Post Office over the counter, on completion of the usual tedious form plus two passport photographs and the sight of your Birth Certificate. This passport is valid for only one year. If you are going to be a constant traveller overseas it pays to obtain a ten year passport. The forms for this are obtainable at most travel agents. Allow at least four weeks.

About to board the ship direct to Spain

The frontier guards seem to think it funnier than does Cyril Ayton

A Hovercraft provides a quick and convenient method of crossing the English Channel

Visas are required for the East Europe countries, except Yugoslavia. Bulgaria does not require a visa for stays of two days and over but otherwise a transit visa is required. Visas are obtainable from the Consular offices of the countries concerned. Most travel agents can organise these for you but, reasonably, you should get your cross-channel tickets from them and they may also make a small charge for this service.

Insurance (Other than vehicle) Comprehensive travel policies which cover loss of personal possessions, including currency and medical fees are available through Insurance Brokers, Banks and Travel Agents. But Insurers do not like motorcycles — and here a majority must pay for the reckless minority — and most exclude injury arising from motorcycling (along, be it said with other hazards such as winter sports) although Car Recovery Service include this with their 'Get You Home Service'. One way to obtain cover is to take out an Annual Accident Policy, which is worth having anyway. Some, but not all, exclude motorcycling and the policy will include cover for trips abroad. See your Broker and read the policy carefully before paying over the premium.

Emergency medical treatment Other countries are far less generous with their medical services available to British nationals than we are to them. The EEC will provide emergency medical treatment if you are armed with Form E111 which you obtain by completing Form CM1 obtainable from the local office of the Department of Health and Social Security. Even this treatment will not necessarily be free (don't ask me to be precise about the meaning of this, I am only quoting what I have been told). Yugoslavia and the other East European countries are much more generous and, so far as I am aware, do not require documentation.

Get you home service The RAC and AA offer a most comprehensive overseas Travel Policy for their members, which includes bringing your vehicle back in the event of it being damaged or broken down beyond reasonable and prompt repair. The service also includes medical costs and loss, provision for hotels and fares home for injured or incapacitated persons. Enquire at your local offices or the Motoring Organisations in person or by post.

A similar service is also available from Car Recovery Service Club, Unit 10, Trumpers Way, Hanwell London, W.7. Ask your travel agent.

WAYS TO REACH EUROPE   SHIPPING TABLE   BY TRAIN (See INLAND TRANSPORT)

Port of Departure	Destination	Operator	Frequency of sailings	Crossing time
Dover	Calais	Sealink	7-9 daily	under 2 hr
Dover	Calais	Townsend Thoresen	6-12 daily	under 2 hr
Dover	Boulogne	Sealink	3-4 daily	under 2 hr
Dover	Boulogne	Normandy/ P & O Ferries	4 daily	under 2 hr
Folkestone	Calais	Sealink	3 daily	under 2 hr
Folkestone	Boulogne	Sealink	2 daily	under 2 hr
Dover	Dunkerque	Sealink	4 daily	3 hours
Dover	Ostend	Sealink	9 daily	3¾ hours
Dover	Zeebrugge	Townsend Thoresen	5 daily	4 hours
Newhaven	Dieppe	Sealink	2-4 daily	3¾ hours
Southampton	Le Havre	Townsend Thoresen	2 or 3 daily	7 hours
Southampton	Cherbourg	Townsend Thoresen	2 daily	7 hours
Portsmouth	Cherbourg	Townsend Thoresen	2 daily	7 hours
Weymouth	Cherbourg	Sealink	1 or 2 peak season	4 hours
Harwich	Hook of Holland	Sealink	2 daily	7 hours
Plymouth	Rostoff (Brittany)	Brittany Ferries	2 daily	7 hours
Hull	Rotterdam	North Sea Ferries	1 daily	Overnight
Newcastle	Norway (various ports)	Fred Olsen	5 weekly	17 - 29 hr
Southampton	Bilbao, Spain	Swedish Lloyd	5 to 7 monthly	1½ days (2 nights)
Southampton	Santander, Spain	Aznar/ P & O	2 weekly	

OTHER SERVICES — HOVERCRAFT

* Ramsgate	Calais	Hoverlloyd	up to 20 daily	40 min
Dover	Calais	Seaspeed	up to 15 daily	30 min

AIRCRAFT

Southend	Rotterdam	British Air Ferries	1 daily	
Southend	Ostend	Britiah Air Ferries	2 daily	
Southend	Le Touquet	British Air Ferries	2 daily	
Southend	Basle	British Air Ferries	1 daily	

* Phone 01-499 9481 for reservations: pay on arrival.

Daily frequency of sailings are for the 24 hour period which may include night crossings.

This does not exhaust the sea crossings which also operate from various ports on the East coast to Germany, Denmark, Holland, and Sweden. Some of these services may be added to, others could be withdrawn, but your travel agent, if he is worth a light, should be able to tell you all the alternatives which might best suit your journey.

One thing to remember, the short channel crossing from Dover or Folkestone is the cheapest way of reaching the Continent (Hovercraft are slightly less still) but in cost per mile they are the most expensive — this is because of high port dues which are the same for a long trip as a short one.

In most cases the wise choice would be determined either by the port of sailing nearest to your home, or the port on the other side which puts you furthest on your way to your intended route or destination — whichever saves the most miles. The extra you might pay for your sea journey might well balance or even exceed the cost of your petrol plus wear and tear — if you are sensible enough to include this figure in your running costs. This is something you must balance up, not forgetting that fuel costs more on the Continent than it does in Britain, so it's best to do your mileage here if it offsets comparable mileage abroad.

It will cost you roughly four times as much to go from Southampton to North Spain as it costs to cross to France on the short crossing. The journey to Spain takes about 36 hours and includes a bunk in a shared cabin for the two nights aboard. But if you want to tour Spain it will not only save you money overall but time as well and so extends your holiday.

Obtaining tickets The easiest way is through your friendly and efficient local travel agency — if he doesn't merit the praise go elsewhere if you have a choice, as most agents strive to give good service. Although a solo motorcycle can always be squeezed aboard a car ferry — providing the traffic controller is not suffering from dyspepsia - the shipping people are somewhat tedious about tying you down to a specific outward crossing although on the short crossing they don't mind issuing an open return ticket. Although there is seldom a reduction for a return ticket — being the same as two singles — it should still save you money as the price is usually more if obtained on the other side but this depends on the vagaries of the rate of exchange for the Pound. If you obtain your ticket on the other side it will come out of your travel allowance and you must allow for a delay while you purchase it and you can lose priority to someone who already has his ticket. On the other hand there is the advantage of being able to keep your options open, depending where you happen to be on your return lap when it might make sense to cross back by a different route. There is, of course, no obstacle to buying one ticket outwards and another inwards, by a different service. Again, discuss the various aspects with your travel agent.

Travel agents abroad tend to be less well versed about the optional services to England so you would be well advised to take a list of the schedules and ports along with you. Even if you feel committed to coming back on a definite sailing it can still be helpful to know the alternatives as, after a two thousand mile or more run, you might be near or far on the final lap, so why hang around or, alternatively, break your neck?

Inland transport Although Motorail services are not available to motorcycles, we are better off. In Britain you may take your motorcycle by rail as accompanied luggage for half the price of the single second class passenger fare but the maximum supplementary charge will not exceed £4 (December 1976 figure). The price is the same for a moped or a quarter ton monster. The vehicle must contain only sufficient fuel to enable it to be ridden to the nearest filling station (how on earth is this decided?).

France A motorcycle may also be taken as accompanied luggage for a supplementary charge.

Other countries in Europe Reasonably presume to offer the same facility.

This is obviously the way to bring back a lame machine if you are not lame yourself. This opens up other prospects too, particularly for owners of lightweights and mopeds. Assuming a moped owner living in London wishes to tour the Scottish Highlands (and why not?): he cannot use the Motorway in any case and it is a long drag so far north, so what better way is there of doing it? Next to a motorcycle I find a fast Intercity train the nicest way to travel. Just wine and dine at a price you can scarcely afford as you slip along at a comfortable 100 mph.

Visitors to Britain Overseas visitors bringing their vehicles with them must, of course, have a passport, a valid driving licence of their own country and third party indemnity insurance for their vehicle as well as their national registration documents giving details of the machine and ownership.

There is a reciprocal arrangement with those countries already listed who recognise a British insurance certificate — in other words their domestic insurance will cover them in Britain for indemnity only, so it is still advised that they obtain a Green Card from their insurers. The Green Card is naturally acceptable for all other nationals. Short term insurance cover is available through the Port Offices or the RAC and AA on arrival, but it is expensive and generally it is better to arrange for cover in your own country.

Medical services available, to visitors to Britain All nationals visiting Britain are entitled to emergency treatment free of charge under the National Health Service. As implied, free treatment is not available for a disorder from which the visitor suffered previously. In the event of injury through accident on the roads, it is probable that no action will be required of the unfortunate as almost certainly someone will communicate with the ambulance service. In the event of injury from other causes, away from onlookers, and it must be serious enough to regard as requiring immediate attention, by dialling 999 on any telephone, public or private, the operator will connect the caller with the Police, Fire or Ambulance service on request and without charge. Free hospital treatment will include everything, accommodation in a ward (not private room), food, medicine and surgical attention, if required, but only for the minimum period deemed necessary before the patient may safely leave or be fit enough to travel back to his or her own country.

For injury, not of a drastic nature, nearly all hospitals have casualty departments, who will render first aid. Hospitals are not always so conveniently close at hand but there are numerous health centres in cities and one in nearly every community. These are listed under National Health Service in the local Telephone Directory. Doctors are listed under Physicians in the Yellow Pages Directories. Most doctors have a surgery or operate in group practices, which function within specific hours and will not normally charge for emergency consultation or treatment. They can also arrange for hospital admission. If a doctor has to be called to visit a patient in bed, they may charge for this at their discretion.

When it comes down to it, it is most unlikely that the stranger in pain who is far from home will be left entirely to organise his own arrangements. Other people will almost certainly come to his aid with practical assistance. In my experience it is the same the world over.

Conversion to metric Most speedometers which record in miles also indicate the kilometres in smaller figures but it is often more useful to be able to calculate the conversion in your head.

As near as makes little difference a Kilometre is 5/8ths of a mile. Divide kilometres by eight, multiply the result by five and here you have your miles. Thus 8 kilometres is five miles. Half of this is 4 kilometres which is 2½ miles or 2.5 miles. You are now equipped for quick mental arithmetic! 80 kilometres is 50 miles, simple, 40 k's is half that, 25. So what is 120 kph? Quick now! 120 is 80 plus 40 — and that is 50 and 25 which together makes 75 mph. You merely have to memorise a few useful multiples of kilometres and their equivalent miles when converting in your head; to reach an approximation becomes easy and is quicker than multiplying 5/8, particularly if you are in movement and preoccupied by other things. If you occupy yourself by converting the distances on the signs as you go along, you'll have memorised the lot when further arithmetical calculation is seldom necessary.

WEIGHT

A thousand grammes to a kilo, a thousand kilos to the tonne. You are not likely to be interested in the latter unless a truck runs over your foot! One Kilo is roughly 2 1/5 lbs. When buying fruit and vegetables it is near enough to think of half kilo being 1 lb. Butter, cold sliced meat and other more expensive foods are available in units of 100 grammes or roughly 3½ oz. Only these few approximations will suffice for your shopping.

MEASURE

The virtue of metrics is the interrelation of volume, distance and weight. A litre of water weighs one kilo, a litre is also 1000 cc. For the practical purposes likely to be involved, one litre is a small quart (when buying oil) and five litres is a large gallon (when filling up).

TYRE PRESSURES

I cannot work out an easily remembered relationship between pounds per square inch and kilos per square centimetre, which is the tedious way that Continentals indicate air pressures, so I must give a table and you had better make a note of the equivalent air pressures your tyres require.

TYRE PRESSURES

Pounds per square inch (psi)	Kilogrammes per square centimetres (kg/cm^2)
14	0.98
16	1.12
18	1.26
20	1.40
22	1.54
24	1.68
26	1.83
28	1.96
30	2.10
32	2.24
36	2.52
40	2.80

TEMPERATURES

The formula for converting Centigrade to Fahrenheit is $^{\circ}C \times \dfrac{9}{5} + 32 = \,^{\circ}F$. An easy way to reach an approximation is to double the Centigrade figure and add 30, or for the other way round, subtract 30 from the F. temperature and divide by two.

16 In times of misfortune

This is not a predictable world, it would be very dull if it were. If you want to lead a secure life, then stay at home and tend the flower gardens for exercise and adventure.

Things have gone drastically wrong. You are in a mountainous country and have mistakenly gone up a dead end track in the fog which has descended with the night. You have run off at the end and the front wheel is inextricably jammed between two boulders, or the machine is immobilised through one thing or another. It is still foggy combined with drizzle, there is no other traffic, no habitation is in sight, you have no tent or if you have there is no ground available where you can pitch it. So what do you do? Much as I shall try to cope with hypothetical problems in this book, you won't find the detailed solution to this situation by hastily turning over the pages while holding it in front of your headlamp which, mercifully, still works. I will now reply to my theoretical question by posing another question "what will this calamity do to you and to your morale?"

Now for the action; dismount and light a cigarette, this being one of the few occasions when a smoking habit is justified. If you don't smoke that's unfortunate, try holding your breath while silently reciting the Lord's Prayer. Now list your blessings — your wife/girlfriend is with you; you haven't been deserted — yet, and meanwhile they are captive through circumstances. You remember you still have half a bar of chocolate and a stale bun so look for it. You suddenly find yourself caught short for a pee — how providential that you should have been brought to a halt at this propitious time. You have now whiled away a few minutes and meanwhile your mind has been working furiously sorting out the options.

In real life there are no square jawed heroes who have all the answers and never inwardly quail. The heroes are the ones who don't display their panic, not only concealing it from others but themselves as well. It has been my observation that most people can behave like heroes in a crisis — that we are equipped with some protective mechanism which becomes progressively effective the more dire the circumstances. I have not had to endure the precise circumstances I have outlined but there have been a few other occasions which have not been dissimilar in their apparent hopelessness.

At least I have the benefit of experience and I'll pass on the encouraging aspects which you can ponder over if your morale ever drops to the bottom of your boots. The extent to which a dire situation can be solved, you can take for granted, is actually going to be achieved as the result of your own efforts, combined with a little good fortune, and you are bound to find enough good fortune when you work for it. Where a calamity is not irreversible you know for sure that in the end you will be nourished, have a warm bed and will be back on the road in due course.

How many times in your life have you said to yourself "if only it were one hour on from now"? Think of the fellow who has absentmindedly wandered into the Ladies changing room at the swimming pool. Too late he becomes aware of his mistake and is forced to take refuge in a cubicle to escape detection. Midst the sounds of girlish laughter from the showers opposite he will pray "Oh Lord, dear Lord, put me on Thy time machine and let it be supper time when I am at home!" So you're lost and forlorn and you know you are going to have to endure some discomfort, uncertainty and frustration before the inevitable solution is found. And now is the time to think how lucky you are not to be the fellow who is stuck in that cubicle in the Ladies changing room!

IN TROUBLE — HELP!

This is really a continuation of the 'mishap in the mountains' saga except that I will envisage that you are now in a position to attract the attention of others.

As a motorcyclist you are a member of the world's largest fraternity. Forgive me if this sounds trite: yachtsmen, mountaineers and other adventurers also look after their own but they are somewhat less numerous, and yachtsmen, in particular, spend most of their time painting or titivating their craft or leaning on their elbows over a pint while discussing spinnakers, caulking and the rest.

This leads me up to an assurance for the timid who have not yet ventured far from home. If you are stranded or in some sort of difficulty, you can be just about certain that another motorcyclist or an ex-motor-cyclist will appear from somewhere to come to your aid. During my many hundreds of thousands of miles I have had my just quota of problems and on every occasion when I have been in desperate need for outside help another motorcyclist has appeared to provide the solution to my problem. I do not suggest you should just sit down and wait for providence to produce the right person from out of the blue, although this will sometimes happen. You may have to take positive steps to attract another rider, particularly on busy urban roads. If you are a pretty lass you hardly have to try at all, though I hope you know a wolf when you see one. Not all motorcyclists are pretty lasses but if you are a mere male transporting a wife or girlfriend, give them the job of standing by the roadside, or whatever the tactical move might be to meet the situation.

Troubles that start off being depressing and distressing will often end up as happy memories because of the people one has met in the process of finding a solution. There was the fellow from Las Vegas with a Harley who helped me cope with some misbehaving electrics in the heat of a desert sun in Arizona — without his more expert knowledge I would have been sunk. From other encounters have developed longer friendships and now I am thinking of Serio and dear Pier of Padova, Eduardo of Lisbon, although I haven't been in touch with him for a few years. These are not the only ones.

It should be a great comfort to know that the further you are from home the greater will be the help you are likely to receive but in accepting it you must also be prepared to give without stint when your turn comes round. Remember to say your thank yous, not everyone does. Take your helper's name and address — if you drop him a line later, that really is appreciated.

YOUR MONEY ABROAD

At the time of writing, British Subjects are restricted to a travel allowance of £300 for each trip they make abroad and it can be more than one trip a year. This is more generous than most people can afford but it is desirable to take a surplus with you for emergencies. The Travel Allowance may be taken in foreign currency or travellers cheques or a combination of both and this is the more usual.

Both are obtainable from banks and you must take your passport with you as the amount issued to you must be recorded on this document. In addition, you are allowed to take with you £25 in Sterling, the idea being that you will need money on your return and it is not intended for your use abroad although, of course, you may change it into foreign currency in the event of an emergency.

This is a typical port side bureau de change, which is combined with an RAC office

This is a typical traveller's cheque kindly loaned by Barclays Bank. They do provide your money with security in a foreign country — they are easy to buy, easy to cash but hard to steal and then cash

Help!

You put your right leg in......

Travellers cheques are generally supplied in Sterling and when changed they realise foreign currency at the prevailing rate of exchange on the day you change them. By advance arrangement you can obtain travellers cheques in the currency of the country you are visiting (only available for main currencies). The only advantage to this is that they are worth a fixed amount and, once purchased, they do not fluctuate in value dependent on the rate of exchange. If the Pound rises in value in the interval you will lose by this process, if it goes down you will gain. Surplus travellers cheques and currency notes (not coins) can be exchanged back on your return. It is not necessary for you to have an account with the bank from which you obtain your cheques and currency. Travellers cheques can be exchanged abroad at almost any bank and all Bureaux de Change, which are open at more convenient hours. There may be a slight difference in the rate paid to you between one place or another. The rates of exchange are normally posted in a prominent place, so you will know what you will be getting, less a small commission. At main railway stations on the Continent you can often change money or cheques at all hours. Large hotels are often willing to change travellers cheques, even for non-residents, but make a high profit at your expense in doing so.

If you have a Post Office account, you can enquire at your Post Office or write to the Accounts Manager, National Giro Centre, Bootle, Lancs. GIROAA, for the free information leaflet on the National Giro International Services. Giro vouchers can be issued which can be cashed in any foreign post office — again highly practical and safe.

Times have changed since these interesting photographs were taken in 1967 although they both illustrate well the problems of breakdown with a motorcycle. Obviously any kind of mechanic, whether he is an RAC employee or not, will first try to get a machine running again. If all is lost then a 'tow' is all that is left

In financial trouble? Your wallet and travellers cheques have been stolen, what now? In the end you can receive reimbursement for the lost travellers cheques but not at once. Somehow manage to telephone or wire home, if you have a friend or family who can help you. They should see your Bank to arrange for emergency funds to be sent to you. If all else fails, you should visit the nearest British Consulate, where you will be sure of a chilly reception. At worst they are compelled to ensure your repatriation (which is more than the Americans will do for their own people) but they will confiscate your passport and send you back the cheapest way, with a one way entry permit. I do not know what their best might be, but have few hopes. The Welfare State is not concerned with your welfare when you are abroad, unless you are the victim of an earthquake or caught up in a revolution. In either of these cases the government might send a sloop or aircraft to evacuate you and your fellow countrymen but say goodbye to your motorcycle. If I speak with cynicism it is backed up with some knowledge, but the British behave no worse or much better to their peoples abroad than other countries.

This doleful prospect has the advantage that it should kindle the spirit of adventure. Once you are out there, boy, you are on your own, like the solitary sailor at sea.

If you have an RAC or AA foreign touring service, you could manage if these documents too are not missing. If nothing else, use your initiative, there must be a solution if you think first and then act. Motorcyclists exist throughout the world — one of them would be happy to have the chance to see you out of trouble. I can't supply the answer, only suggest the precaution. Keep an emergency reserve in a different place so that all at one time is not likely to be lost or stolen.

Appendix 1
1 The incredible hybrid

For many decades the motorcycle and sidecar — combination, combo, rig, outfit, call it what you will — flourished in great numbers as an economical family conveyance. As an utilitarian device it was killed stone dead with the appearance of the Mini and the other small cars that followed since these were far more comfortable and efficient for the functional transport of several people. The sports chair for one just managed to escape extinction, being kept alive by a few enthusiasts, including myself, who loved them for their own very special qualities. Now there are signs of a revival; not in a big way yet, but from now on one is going to see rather more of them about.

A good sporting outfit is not cheap to buy nor particularly economical to run. What then are its special qualities? Not the functional ones on their own, although these are worth mentioning. First of all the chair will provide a degree more comfort for the passenger, in most cases the cherished female, particularly when it rains. They immensely increase luggage carrying capacity, a doubtful virtue as I find that to stow twice as much luggage in twice the available space takes exactly twice as long. From the driver's point of view the combo is a completely different and unique conveyance. First of all it must be consciously steered round the bends, when it leans in the opposite direction to the way one is accustomed on a bike. It is this feature which disconcerts the beginner, compelling him to learn all over again if his nerve survives the first encounter.

I think I would be right in saying that driving an outfit requires more developed skill and more continuous concentration than any other road vehicle. Perhaps it is the challenge that adds to its charm. After all, it is surely the challenge and the need to extend oneself that adds the punch to skiing, tennis, mountaineering or other sports which require dedication to be able to do them reasonably well.

After all that, you don't have to be highly skilled to drive an outfit competently, but you will be missing out by remaining mediocre and once they really get hold of you, there is nothing for it but to accept the challenge and go on to be able to take advantage of their full potential. Once you have become the master of this asymmetrical contraption, which has all of the power and much of the weight offset to one side, you can challenge the solos on the mountain bends and then cope with road conditions which no other standard vehicle could hope to emulate. It can be taken through floods, over dreadful surfaces and up nigh impossible slopes. As a winter sports device it stands right out on its own, hence the popularity of the Elephant Rally which draws out the combos, like an impulsive annual migration, to the Hartz mountains in January. All over Europe they will be seen and heard as they swish over snow covered and icebound roads. At speed they will drift widely when rounding the bends, but when you know what you are doing they will remain fully under control as their behaviour is predictable. They are the nearest thing yet to a non-skid vehicle.

I tended to favour the combination for most of our long tours abroad but not to the exclusion of a solo. I love them both dearly for their own different virtues.

Unfortunately it is not very practical to use one mount in a dual role. The sidecar machine needs heavier springs in both front and rear telescopic suspensions or it will bottom repeatedly. The gearing needs to be reduced by fitting a smaller engine sprocket and unless the motorcycle is fitted with a steering damper it can go into a tank slapping wobble at (mercifully) lower speeds. There is nothing for it but to have one of each in the stable, as I had. This is an expensive business — I couldn't really afford them either — but the trouble is that once you are hooked on both you are left with no option.

Bill Peacock suffers in silence whilst he coaxes Ken Craven through a deep water splash

Britain's only production sidecar? The Squire attached to a Honda 750 Four

When the going is really bad a third wheel can be a real help

A motorcycle and sidecar makes an ideal winter sports vehicle

Seemingly still done in America, caravan towing has disappeared in Europe. Here Roger Maughfling and Ken Craven, on their way to Monte Carlo, high in the Italian Alps, give their Matchless a rest

Appendix 2
European
mountain passes

PASS	HEIGHT IN FEET	COUNTRY	ROAD	CONDITION IN WINTER
Albula	7,595	Switzerland	63 Tiefencastel to La Punt	Closed Nov - June
Allos	7,382	France	D908 Barcelonnette to Entrevauy	Closed Nov - May
Argentera Arlberg	5,912	Austria	190 Feldkirch to Innsbruck	Intermittent closure
AuBisque	5,611	France	N618 Laruns to Argeles-Gazost	Closed Nov - June
Bernina	7,644	Italy/Switzerland	29 Celerina to Tirano	Closed Nov - mid May
Bielerhohe Bonaigua	6,798	Spain	C142 Esterri de Aneo to Viella	Closed Oct - May
Campolongo	6,151	Italy	244 Coruaro to Arabba	Intermittent closure
Cayolle	7,632	France	D902 Barcelonnete to Nice	Closed Nov - mid June
Costalunga	5,752	Italy	241 Cortina to Bolzano	Intermittent closure
Croix de ger	6,785	France	NS26 la Mure to St. Jean de Maurienne	Closed Oct - June
Envalira	7,897	Andorra	N8 L'Hospitalet to Andorra	Closed Nov - May
Falzarego	6,905	Italy	48 Ora to Cortina	Intermittent closure between Nov and June
Felbertavern	5,414	Austria	108 Mittersil to Lienz	Open
Flexen	5,853	Austria	198 Stuben to Reutte	Intermittent closure
Fluela	7,815	Switzerland	28 Landquart to Susch	Closed Nov - May
Forclaz	5,010	Switzerland	115 Martigny to Chamonix	Closed Nov - late May
Furka	7,976	Switzerland	19 Andermatt to Brig	Closed Nov mid June
Galibier	8,386	France	N202 St. Michael de Maurienne to Lauteret Saddle	Closed mid Oct - late June
Gardena	6,957	Italy	243 Selva to Corvara	Closed Dec - April
Gavid	8,600	Italy	300 Bormio to Ponte di Legno	Closed Dec - May
Gerlos Platte	5,341	Austria	165 Zell am Ziller to Mittersill	
Great St. Bernard	8,114	Italy/Switzerland	21127 Martigny to Aosta	Closed Oct - June except through tunnel
Grimsel	7,100	Switzerland	6 Gletsch to Innertkirchen	Closed late Oct - early June
Gross Glockner	8,212	Austria	107 Bruck to Lienz	Closed Oct - late May
Hochtannberg	5,512	Austria	200 Egg to Warth	Closed Nov - April
Iseran	9,088	France	N202 Lanslebourg to Bourg St. Maurice	Closed Oct - late June

PASS	HEIGHT IN FEET	COUNTRY	ROAD	CONDITION IN WINTER
Izoard	7,743	France	N202 Briancon to Guillestre	Closed late Oct - early June
Julier	7,493	Switzerland	3 Tiefencasrel to Silvaplana	Intermittent closure
Karschberg	5,384	Austria	99 Spittal to Roadstradr	Intermittent closure
Klausen	6,390	Switzerland	17 Alrdorg to Glarus	Closed early Nov - early June
Larche	6,545	France/Italy	21 Cuneo to Barcelonnette	Closed Nov - May
Lautaret	6,751	France	N91 Briancon to Nizille	Intermittent closure
Leitariegos	5,004	Spain	C.C631 Ponterrada to La Espina	Intermittent closure
Lukmanier	6,286	Switzerland	61 Disentis to Biasca	Closed Nov - mid May
Maloja	5,960	Italy/Switzerland	3 Chiavenna to Silvaplana	Intermittent closure
Mt. Cenis	6,834	France/Italy	N6 Chamberg to Turin	Closed late Nov - late May
Mt. Genevre	6,083	France/Italy	N94/24 Braincon to Turin	Usually open
Monte Goivo	6,870	Italy	44 Merano to Vipiteno	Closed Nov - early May
Navacerrada	6,103	Spain	N601 Madrid to Segovia	Intermittent closure
Nufenen	8,131	Switzerland	Brig to Airolo	Closed late Oct - early June
Oberalp	6,706	Switzerland	19 Andermatt to Disentis	Closed late Nov - early May
Ozen	7,006	Switzerland	28 Zernez to Santa Maria	Closed late Nov - early May
Petit St. Bernard	7,179	France/Italy	90 Bourg St. Maurice to Aosta	Closed Oct - mid June
Peyresourde	5,128	France	N618 Arreau to Bagneres de Luchon	Closed Dec - late March
Pillon	5,072	Switzerland	20 Aigle to Saanen	Closed Oct - May
Pordoi	7,356	Italy	48 Arabba to Canazei	Closed Nov - May
Pourtalet	5,889	France/Spain	N134/C136 Pau to Huesca	Closed Nov - early June
Paymorens	6,283	France	N20 Toulouse to Bourg Madame	Closed Nov - mid May
Quillane	5,653	France	N118 Carcassonne to Mount Louis	Closed Nov - March
Restegond	8,786	France	D64 Jausiers to St. Etienne de Tinee	Closed Oct - late June
Rolle	6,464	Italy	50 Predazzo to Primiero	Closed Nov - May
San Bernardino	6,778	Switzerland	13 Chur to Bellinzona	Closed Nov - late May
Sella	7,349	Italy	242 Ortisei to Canazei	Closed Nov - March
Sestriere	6,670	Italy	23 Cesana Torinese to Turin	Usually open
Silvretta	6,679	Austria	188 Bluden to Landeck	Closed Nov - May
Simplon	6,591	Italy/Switzerland	Domodossola	Intermittent closure
Somport	5,380	Spain	N.330/N.134 Pau to Zaragoza	Closed Nov - mid May
Splugen	6,949	Italy/Switzerland	36 Splugen to Chaivenna	Closed Nov - May
St. Gotthard	6,929	Switzerland	2 Andermatt to Bellinzona	Closed Oct - May
Stelvio	9,049	Italy	38 Bormio to Spondigno	Closed mid Oct - late June
Susten	7,300	Switzerland	11 Innerkirchen to Wassen	Closed late Oct - mid June
Timmels Zoch	8,237	Austria	186/446 Otz to Merano	Closed Oct - mid June
Tonale	6,181	Italy	42 Edolo to Bolzano	Closed Dec - April
Tosas	5,906	Spain	N.152 Barcelona to Puigcerda	Usually open
Trecroci	5,935	Italy	48 Cortina to Auronzo	Closed Nov - May

PASS	HEIGHT IN FEET	COUNTRY	ROAD	CONDITION IN WINTER
Turracher Howe	5,784	Austria	95 Predlitz to Feldkerchen	Intermittent closure
Umbrail	8,212	Italy/Switzerland	66 Santa Maria to Bormio	Closed late Oct - mid June
Vars	6,939	France	D902/N202 Barcelonnette to Guillestre	Closed Nov - April